COMPANY IN YOUR CLASSROOM

Building a Learning Relationship with Your Student Teacher

DEVELOPMENTAL STUDIES CENTER

Developmental Studies Center
2000 Embarcadero, Suite 305
Oakland, CA 94606-5300
(800) 666-7270 / (510) 533-0213

Funding to support the development, piloting, and dissemination of
Developmental Studies Center programs has been provided by the following:

The Annenberg Foundation, Inc.
Anonymous Donor
The Robert Bowne Foundation, Inc.
The Annie E. Casey Foundation
Center for Substance Abuse Prevention
   Substance Abuse and Mental Health
   Services Agency, U.S. Department of
   Health and Human Services
The Danforth Foundation
The Ford Foundation
Evelyn and Walter Haas, Jr. Fund
J. David & Pamela Hakman Family Foundation
Charles Hayden Foundation
The William Randolph Hearst Foundation
Clarence E. Heller Charitable Foundation
The William and Flora Hewlett Foundation
The James Irvine Foundation
The Robert Wood Johnson Foundation
Walter S. Johnson Foundation
Ewing Marion Kauffman Foundation
W.K. Kellogg Foundation
John S. and James L. Knight Foundation
Lilly Endowment, Inc.
The MBK Foundation

Mr. & Mrs. Sanford N. McDonnell
The John D. and Catherine T. MacArthur
   Foundation
A.L. Mailman Family Foundation, Inc.
Charles Stewart Mott Foundation
National Institute on Drug Abuse
   (NIDA), National Institutes of Health
National Science Foundation
Nippon Life Insurance Foundation
The Pew Charitable Trusts
The Pinkerton Foundation
The Rockefeller Foundation
Louise and Claude Rosenberg, Jr.
The San Francisco Foundation
Shinnyo-En Foundation
The Spencer Foundation
Spunk Fund, Inc.
Stuart Foundation
The Stupski Family Foundation
The Sulzberger Foundation, Inc.
Surdna Foundation, Inc.
DeWitt Wallace–Reader's Digest Fund
Wells Fargo Bank

Contents

A third-grader on the first day of the student teacher's takeover:

"Okay, Ms. Henry, whatever happens, don't get upset. Stay calm!"

Preface

THIS HANDBOOK IS DESIGNED TO HELP YOU, AS A CLASSROOM TEACHER, work effectively with a student teacher. It focuses on the ongoing mentoring relationship you establish with your student teacher—the day-to-day relationship that falls largely on your shoulders. Even if you are working closely with your student teacher's university-based supervisor, you are the person who is with the student teacher in the classroom every day, you are the person who can provide on-the-spot support and feedback, and you are the person whose classroom will thrive or falter—perhaps because of your success or failure communicating with your student teacher and integrating him or her into your classroom community. Because of the uniqueness of your role and the magnitude of your responsibility, there may be times when you feel isolated or unsure of how best to support your student teacher. It is our hope that this handbook can help.

Besides providing concrete ideas and practical tools for working with a student teacher, this handbook brings you the voices and experiences of other mentoring teachers—and their student teachers. Both sets of perspectives can help you anticipate and understand the pleasures and challenges of mentoring the hopeful but unseasoned teacher-to-be in your care.

In personal interviews, meetings, and university classes, the "informants" for this handbook reflected on what would be most important to communicate to you, based on their own experiences and learning. We hope you will enjoy their insights and honesty.

Working with the Student Teacher's University Program

Since teacher preparation programs differ in how they work with schools and in how student teachers' university-based supervisors work with mentoring teachers (and even in the name they assign to your role—"cooperating," "master," or "mentor" teacher, for example), we have only a few general suggestions about your role in relationship to your student teacher's teacher preparation program.

We do suggest that you work out your role as mentoring teacher with the university program and that you involve your student teacher's university-based supervisor in initial goal setting and ongoing discussions of any concerns you may have about the student teacher's progress. In the event that you and your student teacher have serious disagreements or you find yourself at a loss for how to help the student progress, it would be especially important to ask for the university supervisor's involvement. But even when everything is going fine, it is important for you to understand the goals and expectations of your student teacher's university program so that you are better prepared to help the student teacher achieve those goals and so that you can provide feedback and advice to the teacher preparation program.

The Educational Philosophy Reflected in This Handbook

This handbook is one of many print and video teacher resources created by Developmental Studies Center. DSC is a nonprofit educational organization established in 1980 to conduct research and develop learner-centered programs that foster caring and integrate children's intellectual, social, and ethical development. Our mission is to deepen children's commitment to values such as kindness, helpfulness, personal responsibility, and respect for others, and to help children develop their capacities to think deeply and critically so that they can continue learning throughout their lives.

The educational philosophy represented in DSC materials is based on two decades of research and collaboration with teachers, students, parents, and administrators in schools across the country. At its core is a belief that providing for children's autonomy, sense of belonging, and competence is the most decent and productive way to challenge and support their development—and that their development as learners, social beings, and ethical citizens is best approached as an integrated whole.

The Classroom Management Approach Reflected in This Handbook

When DSC's educational philosophy is applied to classroom management, the goal is to create a caring learning community. Achieving such a community is one of the hardest challenges student teachers and beginning teachers face. It can take years for even the most highly skilled teacher to develop a comfortable, effective management style that supports children and their learning without relying on undue control, punishments, or rewards.

Because the definition of "undue" can be a slippery one, it may be easier to understand the classroom management approach in this book by first identifying the two general approaches to classroom management represented in most American classrooms. If we boil down the many existing approaches or systems for classroom management and discipline, the two types are differentiated in the following important ways:

- the relative importance of their goals,
- their assumptions about children's motivation, and
- the techniques they suggest for achieving a harmonious classroom.

Two General Approaches to Classroom Management		
	1	**2**
Goals	primarily academic	integration of academic, social, and ethical
Motivation Assumptions	primarily self-interest	self-interest plus intrinsic motivation to learn and make positive contributions to others
Techniques for Achieving Harmony	teacher control plus rewards/punishments	teacher control plus teaching the skills of self-control

One type of classroom management assumes that the primary or only goal of schooling is academic learning, and that children's social and ethical development, while important, is the responsibility of family or family and church or other religious institution. Those who embrace such a set of assumptions usually view the goal of classroom management as controlling children's social behavior in order to maximize the learning time for academic subjects.

Often underlying such systems is an assumption about children's motivations—an assumption that children are primarily motivated by self-interest. Thus, if we want children to act in certain ways, we need to show them that it is in their self-interest to act in those ways, and not in their self-interest to act in other ways.

Following from this assumption, these systems rely primarily on rewards and punishments to control children's behavior. Through the years such systems have developed increasingly efficient ways to control behavior by dispensing rewards and punishments. Lee Cantor's "Assertive Discipline" is the quintessential example of this approach to discipline and classroom management.

A second approach to classroom management and discipline assumes that children's social and ethical development is as important a goal of schooling as their intellectual development, even though this responsibility is shared with family or family and church.

Complementing this second goal is the assumption that children, while motivated by self-interest, are also internally motivated to learn and to be good people.

Proponents of this second approach understand the need to control children's behavior and the importance of providing a climate conducive to strong academic learning, but they also see the importance of taking the time needed to foster children's social and ethical understanding and to help them develop the skills needed to assume responsibility for their own behavior. Furthermore, since ethical development necessarily involves acting for the good of others or in accord with internally held moral principles, proponents of this approach cannot rely primarily or exclusively on self-interest for motivation; ethical development requires that one become committed to doing what is right regardless of self-interest.

This second approach—though far more complicated for student teachers to learn and implement—is what this handbook is about. It requires the teacher to know how to control children's behavior when needed, but it further requires the teacher to know how to develop children's understanding of what it is to be a good person, their commitment each to be such a person, and the skills to succeed in their efforts. Embedded in this approach is the belief that social learning and academic learning go hand in hand and that both are needed to run an effective, caring classroom and to prepare children to become responsible citizens in a democratic society.

Some of the teachers whose voices run throughout this handbook do not use extrinsic controls—that is, rewards and punishments. Some do. But for those who do, these methods are a very small part of their overall approach to classroom management. Similarly, some of the student teachers who contributed their stories to this handbook reported short-term successes using strategies such as writing names on the board and revoking privileges. Yet they tried to do this with a minimal use of power assertion because their overriding goal was to help students become more responsible for themselves and their learning.

What unites all the teachers you will meet in this handbook is a commitment to building a caring community, to treating all children with love and affection, and to taking the time to build their students' understanding and skills in the moral and social domains, as well as academically.

Acknowledgements and Thanks

For their invaluable contribution to this book, in particular we would like to thank a group of five caring and dedicated teachers who work with student teachers from the University of California at Berkeley's Developmental Teacher Education (DTE) program. Over the course of a school year they opened their classrooms to us and met monthly with us to reflect on the role of the cooperating teacher. It was these student-teacher mentors—Jamie Carlson, Glendi Henion-Ul, Susan Hodges, Lyn Bajai, and Hazelle Fortich—who ultimately shaped the contents of this handbook, along with Laura Ecken, a cooperating teaching in Louisville, Kentucky.

The student teachers, whose comments and experiences interject the crucial "other side" of the story, were enrolled in teacher education programs at the University of California at Berkeley, California State University at Sacramento, and the University of Louisville. We thank them for their openness in sharing their experiences, successes, challenges, and insights. Their sensitivity and ability to reflect on their practice will surely help them to become outstanding mentoring teachers themselves some day.

We are grateful in many ways to Paul Ammon, director of the Developmental Teacher Education program at U.C. Berkeley. Paul has been a thoughtful advisor to DSC's Preservice Initiative, which sponsored the development of this book. He has provided ongoing support and guidance and made it possible for Marilyn Watson to teach—and learn—in the DTE program. He also responded with helpful comments to an earlier draft of this handbook.

This book was written by Marilyn Watson and Amy Schoenblum. Lynn Murphy was its developmental editor and Mark Woodworth its copyeditor. Allan Ferguson was the book's designer, with desktop publishing handled by Leigh McLellan and cover design by Visual Strategies. Photographs are by Jim Ketsdever.

1

Communicating Your Classroom Management Strategy

I F WE BELIEVE THAT CHILDREN'S SOCIAL AND ETHICAL LEARNING ARE as important as their academic learning, then developing a moral classroom community must be approached purposefully. Otherwise, it simply will not happen. Be explicit with your student teacher about everything you do that contributes to a moral classroom and why it is so important—to you and and to the students.

The Importance of Community

The success of our society depends on helping young people develop into citizens who live full and productive lives and contribute to the common good. In a humane democracy, this means helping children embrace the ethics and values that unite us as a society.

Regardless of whether children learn humane values at home, their membership in a caring, or "moral," classroom and school community provides a strong foundation for their development as responsible, caring people.

Just as anyone who feels part of a community will uphold the values of that community and promote the well-being of its members, the more children feel that their school community cares about them and meets their needs, the more likely they are to feel attached to that community, to practice the values it promotes, and to thrive academically and socially.

Creating a classroom in which all members are valued, and in which all members treat all others with fairness, kindness, and respect is a tall order. Not only do teachers have to hold themselves to the highest moral standards, but they must also have to teach sometimes quite reluctant students the skills and understandings they need in order to act in fair and caring ways. And they need to create the conditions that support and require such behavior.

Research Finds Many Student Benefits

While creating caring communities in schools and classrooms is neither automatic nor easy, it is well worth the effort, for students in such communities acquire the values, sensitivities, motives, and skills that are central to good character (Battistich et al., 1997[*]). For example, children who describe their schools and classrooms as caring communities show greater

- empathy with others' feelings,

---

[*] Victor Battistich, Daniel Solomon, Marilyn Watson, and Eric Schaps, "Caring School Communities," *Educational Psychologist,* 32 (1997), 137–151.

- concern for others,
- enjoyment in helping others learn,
- motivation to be kind and helpful to others, and
- ability to resolve conflicts fairly and without force.

They also more frequently engage in helpful behavior on their own initiative—with no promise of reward—and commit fewer acts of delinquent behavior.

This kind of good character indicates a commitment to a set of core values that translate into caring about others as well as oneself, being aware of the needs and feelings of others, understanding the moral implications of one's actions, possessing self-control and skills to act in ways that benefit others, and doing so out of concern for others and a desire to behave in fair, kind, responsible, and honest ways. When people of good character *do* harm others, they try to repair or make up for any distress they have caused, not out of fear of punishment or the promise of reward, but out of concern for the welfare of others and a commitment to core values.

Teachers Find Many Personal Rewards

Classroom life offers unlimited opportunities for children to learn and practice such values and habits. Yet taking advantage of these situations requires a great deal of teacher time and energy, much of which is neither budgeted for nor appreciated. Teachers typically are acknowledged and credited for their students' academic success, but seldom are they recognized for their role in their students' social and ethical development—but this doesn't keep teachers from taking on this vital aspect of their students' development.

Managing a moral classroom requires building and maintaining—with each child—a personal relationship that brings with it all the demands of any personal relationship: children's lives pull at teachers' heartstrings and are never really out of their minds. All the same, because children return such love and affection, teaching in this personal way is usually found to be rewarding.

Building personal relationships and a feeling of community in order to help children become the best learners and people they can be also means working collaboratively with them. Most teachers report that it is more satisfying to work *with* children rather than to control, threaten, or bribe them to get them to behave in accord with standards that have not become their own.

Teacher Competencies That Promote Community

So what do student teachers need to learn in order to be able to create moral classrooms, caring learning communities? Fundamentally, they need to understand teaching as a moral act. They need to believe that as teachers, their role is to help children develop their hearts as well as their minds. Pragmatically, they also need to develop the competencies that allow them to manage classrooms that are safe, caring, and challenging.

If we assume that a student teacher is trying to develop a just and caring learning community—a safe place where children practice shared values and are engaged in meaningful and relevant learning experiences—then he or she is striving to develop personal competence in at least four important areas:

- building relationships with students,
- establishing authority and control of the classroom,
- making the values clear and consistent, and
- engaging every learner.

(Concrete examples of practices that promote these four areas of competence make up "A Reflection Guide for Teachers," which appears on page 87. Although the reflection guide was not developed specifically for this book, it is a concrete way for teachers and student teachers to evaluate practices they use or could use to foster a caring classroom learning community. You may find it a helpful resource in working with your student teacher.)

Building Relationships with Students

To feel safe and supported as learners and as people, students need to know that their teacher is a member of their community as well as its leader—in other words, he or she is a leader who cares about them, is interested in their lives and experiences, and shares his or her own. For a student teacher, this means understanding the nature and role of interpersonal relationships in classroom learning and being able to cross barriers of class, race, language, and personality to form a supportive relationship with each child.

Establishing Authority and Control of the Classroom

Children in a caring learning community take a lot of responsibility for their own learning and behavior, but they also need to know that the teacher, as an authority, will keep the room emotionally and physically safe for every child. When students feel confident that they won't get hurt or teased, they can focus on learning. For a student teacher, the challenge is to establish authority and control without giving up the important goals of being caring and fair.

Making the Values Clear and Consistent

Students need to understand the values that are important to the classroom community and see them applied consistently and fairly. By articulating the class's values, helping children develop positive relationships with each other, and encouraging them to practice the values in their interactions with each other, a student teacher can help build democratic principles into classroom life. As the students' model, the student teacher must build his or her understanding of how these values apply to the teaching role and must strive to live up to these norms and values in his or her own daily actions.

Engaging Every Learner

When the curriculum is interesting, relevant, challenging, and fun, and when students are invited to draw on their backgrounds and prior experiences and make choices about their learning, the classroom is enhanced both intellectually and socially. For a student teacher, this means trying to structure academic learning experiences that tap children's natural motivation to learn and discover and that engage a range of learning styles and skills.

Developing Automaticity

No teacher, however well trained and intentioned, walks into a classroom with all of these skills tucked neatly under his or her belt. Teachers develop them over time—attaining a certain level of "automaticity," or the ability to respond, not automatically or without thought, but quickly and consistently to the hundreds of situations requiring split-second decisions about learning and getting along together in a lively classroom. Student teachers are working at developing this important ability to quickly judge each situation and respond in ways that support children and are consistent with the values of the classroom. It takes time and practice.

As someone who has spent years developing this kind of fluency, you are in a perfect position to help a student teacher understand why these four areas of competence are important goals and how they play out in day-to-day classroom life, as well as to reflect on his or her progress in each area. Your role is also to help the student teacher see that he or she is developing antennae to recognize situations that present teaching opportunities and the ability to respond quickly to them and in sync with his or her principles. From experience, you can also help your student teacher see that each situation is unique and that there is no magic bullet or single response that works from situation to situation, no matter how similar one situation may seem to another. Helping your student teacher understand the underlying similarities between what appear to be different actions—and the underlying differences between what appear to be similar actions—takes a lot of explaining and is one of the major challenges of your role.

> "The amazing thing about teaching is that there are a thousand-and-one different ways to respond to any situation, and you have to be able to draw on them all. You can't just do the same thing every time and expect it to work." (COOPERATING TEACHER)

2

An Overview of Your Relationship with the Student Teacher

AS A COOPERATING TEACHER, YOU WEAR MANY HATS: AS A ROLE MODEL, a coach, an observer, a problem solver, a teacher, and, at times, a friend. As refreshing and fulfilling as it can be to have a student teacher to work with, it also takes time and energy. Having a student teacher in your classroom means spending time with that person—whenever you can snatch a moment as well as on a regular basis—to plan, reflect, share observations, and offer guidance.

For the student teacher, entering your classroom is an adjustment, too. Not only does he or she have to adjust to the group of children and your style as a teacher, but most likely the student teacher is a newcomer in a community where personal relationships have already been formed.

To complicate matters, an inherent inequality exists in the relationship between student teachers and cooperating teachers. Although it is important to stay open to the new ideas and personal insights that your student teacher may bring and the research and strategies that may flow to you from your student teacher's university program, you and your student teacher are *not* equal. Your ability to recognize that inequality, accept the responsibility that it brings, and strive as much as possible for a collaborative and respectful relationship will be key to a successful working alliance.

The student teacher, too, needs to recognize the inequality in your relationship and accept your authority to make decisions regarding the classroom, the children, and ground rules for both. As a guest in your classroom, the student teacher needs to understand his or her professional obligation to support your authority and values.

In the vignettes that follow, cooperating teachers and student teachers describe a wide range of experiences—positive, negative, and confusing. We have included them all to help you remember why you take on the responsibility of a student teacher and to support you in being both forthright and sensitive in negotiating differences when they arise.

As a cooperating teacher who was once a student teacher, you have the advantage of relating to many of the stories below from *both* perspectives.

COOPERATING TEACHER **BENEFITS**

PRACTICAL HELP

▶ Having another perspective on children and situations

▶ Having additional interests or strengths represented

▶ Having another educator to work with children

PROFESSIONAL BOOST

▶ Forcing a clarification of goals and assessment

▶ Having a source of fresh ideas and new thinking in the field

▶ Making possible the rewards of mentorship

STUDENT TEACHER **BENEFITS**

PRACTICAL HELP

▶ Having a laboratory for learning pedagogy

▶ Having a laboratory for learning classroom management

▶ Having someone to share the load

PROFESSIONAL BOOST

▶ Having an accomplished mentor

▶ Having a supportive mentor

▶ Having a colleague in learning

COOPERATING TEACHER **CHALLENGES**

PROFESSIONAL CHALLENGES

▶ Needing to compensate if children are learning less

▶ Deciding what to do if practices conflict

▶ Needing to intervene if children are feeling unsafe

PERSONAL CHALLENGES

▶ Feeling judged

▶ Having relationships with children change

▶ Feeling the responsibility to give honest, constructive feedback even when it might be hard for the student teacher to hear

STUDENT TEACHER **CHALLENGES**

PROFESSIONAL CHALLENGES

▶ Being a guest in someone else's classroom

▶ Deciding what to do if practices conflict

▶ Having authority undermined

PERSONAL CHALLENGES

▶ Believing that one's ideas are being dismissed

▶ Dealing with rivalries

▶ Asking for and getting honest, useful feedback

The Benefits for You

Although the distinctions sometimes blur, it may help to think of the benefits of having a student teacher as both instrumentally and personally valuable—or in terms of the practical help and the professional boost your student teacher can provide.

Practical Help

- Having another perspective on children and situations
- Having additional interests or strengths represented
- Having another educator to work with children

Professional Boost

- Forcing a clarification of goals and assessment
- Having a source of fresh ideas and new thinking in the field
- Making possible the rewards of mentorship

Because teachers so often work alone with a class, having another professional in the room brings with it the welcome benefit of another person thinking about and interacting with the children.

Having Another Perspective on Children and Situations

Cooperating teachers appreciate the presence of another set of eyes and ears helping to identify the needs or problems of individual children. An observant student teacher can also highlight a classroom dynamic that might otherwise go unnoticed.

> "My student teacher always helped pass out student work before the children were picked up by their parents. He noticed that one little girl never took anything home. It's the kind of thing I hadn't noticed because I'm always rushing around: 'You want it? No? Okay. Next? Whose is this? Okay. Good-bye!' He came to me and asked if I had noticed that Jalene wouldn't take her things home. I decided to talk with Jalene and see if I could find out what was going on. I couldn't really get to the bottom of it, but I stopped pushing her to take her things home. Instead I made a special space in the room for her to put up her work. She's very happy to do this and nobody else feels it's unfair because they can put their work up, too, if they wish. Without my student teacher, it would have been easy for me to miss this child." (COOPERATING TEACHER)

"The girls in my classroom seemed a little on edge, but I didn't really think much about it. However, Christy, my student teacher, was in the habit of eating lunch in the cafeteria with the children and witnessed an incident that confirmed what she suspected—that one girl, Richelle, was actively trying to break up existing friendships and was giving and withdrawing her friendship as a means of controlling the others. Once Christy pointed out this pattern to me, I realized that I was seeing it as well but hadn't put it together. Once I was aware of the pattern, I could put a stop to it and help Richelle find a more constructive way to form relationships."
(COOPERATING TEACHER)

Having Additional Strengths or Interests Represented

Children benefit when student teachers have particular strengths or extra energy for a project about something that is a special interest of theirs.

"When we were studying the human body and working on the five senses, my student teacher set up five tables with all this stuff she brought in to help kids experience the five senses. At the 'sound' table—she had recorded all these sounds at home—the kids had to listen and write down what they thought the sounds were. And for touch she brought in feathers and sandpaper and very small, smooth rocks. She had the kids move from table to table in small groups, and it was so interesting to see the whole hands-on thing come alive." (COOPERATING TEACHER)

"My student teacher and the kids transformed the whole classroom into a lush tropical rainforest—a project I couldn't have managed to pull together on my own." (COOPERATING TEACHER)

Having Another Educator to Work with Children

It's not possible for one teacher to spend the time he or she would like to with every student. Having a student teacher in the room can mean more help for more children.

"At the beginning of the year my student teacher offered to pull out and test five of my low readers while I was teaching the rest of the class. The results of her testing gave me valuable in-depth information about these children right when I needed it." (COOPERATING TEACHER)

"When I was student teaching, one child in the class had a very difficult time with collaborative work and building peer relationships in general. Every day Andrew asked me to stay in at recess with him. Although I did not mind spending the time with him, I was reluctant initially, wondering how he would ever make friends with his classmates if he always stayed in with me. So I asked him to invite some of his classmates to stay in with us—this way he could be with a small group and I could help facilitate his interactions. Over time he learned what it means to be a friend. He began going to music class with a partner and learning the excitement of a new friendship as well as a new instrument." (STUDENT TEACHER)

The idea that an inexperienced student teacher can provide a professional boost to a cooperating teacher is sometimes overlooked. Many things, though, can enhance your professional growth: the fresh ideas of a student teacher, your responsibility to act as a role model, and the rewards of experiencing yourself as someone who can help others grow.

Forcing a Clarification of Goals and Assessment

Having to articulate to a student teacher the reasons behind classroom practices—many of which you may have taken for granted—can be a good opportunity to reassess your practices and sharpen your focus on what you want children to learn and how you will know they are getting there.

"It's good for me to have to justify how I spent the day and to try to show how I'm assessing children's progress. It's exhausting, actually! But it keeps me on my toes." (COOPERATING TEACHER)

Having a Source of Fresh Ideas and New Thinking in the Field

Student teachers are eager to bring with them all that they are learning. Your student teacher can be a source of new ways of thinking about curriculum and teaching.

"My student teacher taught me a lot about getting students to write. For example, my fifth graders had not been comfortable writing about thoughts and feelings, but he was able to develop their interest in expressing themselves by having the kids make beautiful hardbound books for their poetry. Once they made their books, they were really excited to fill them." (COOPERATING TEACHER)

"I always thought that letting kids choose their own groups was empowering for them. And I think it is, in a lot of ways, but it was my only method for putting kids in groups. My student teacher asked me one day if I ever made random groups or selected the groups myself. It got me thinking about it, and I realized that there are a lot of benefits to putting kids in groups in different ways. It made me think about how cliques are such a problem in fifth grade, and how I could start to break them up by helping students learn to work with everyone else in the class." (COOPERATING TEACHER)

Making Possible the Rewards of Mentorship

It can be very fulfilling to mentor a student teacher and see him or her develop a strong presence, caring relationships with children, and new skills as a teacher. In addition to all the work of mentoring, as a cooperating teacher you can enjoy the pleasures of contributing to a new teacher's growth.

"My student teacher had a really tough time at first—she struggled with classroom management, having a presence, and demanding respect. During her takeover, I met her in the lunchroom to check in and see how things were going. While we were talking, a third grader from another class ran by. The student teacher immediately turned around and asked the child to go back and walk. It showed that she had become confident enough to correct a child who wasn't even from her class—it was really exciting to see." (COOPERATING TEACHER)

"My children love to lie down when they listen to chapter books, but it's not something they can do without a lot of help controlling themselves. I don't automatically let them do it—each time I read I make a judgment call depending on whether I have the energy to help them manage. One day I walked into the room during my student teacher's takeover and every child was lying on the rug, listening to him read. Obviously he had made the call to let them lie down. Every little body was respectfully not bugging any other body and it was very quiet as he read. I just know how hard he must have worked to get to this place and how good it must have felt to him." (COOPERATING TEACHER)

"My cooperating teacher was a wonderful model. In my teaching now I work a lot with the things I saw her do. I make sure things are fair. I have class meetings and student-of-the-week displays. I have lots of time for kids to share—in her room it seemed so important for the kids to be able to share, so we do that in our room, too. And she was very serious about their learning. That's one thing she wouldn't compromise on, and I try to put that philosophy into my room." (FIRST-YEAR TEACHER)

The Challenges for You

As with the benefits of having a student teacher, the associated strains fall into two broad areas—things that challenge you professionally and things that may be personally difficult to deal with or accept.

Professional Challenges

- Needing to compensate if children are learning less
- Deciding what to do if practices conflict
- Needing to intervene if children are feeling unsafe

Personal Challenges

- Feeling judged
- Accepting that relationships with children have changed
- Shouldering the responsibility to give honest, constructive feedback even when it might be hard for the student teacher to hear

Student teachers are, by definition, learning how to become teachers. They take too long to do some things, fail to give some activities the time they need, make mistakes, and sometimes even let the classroom become unsafe emotionally or physically. When you see any of this happening, it can set up a tension about what you should do in the moment and what you may have to do later.

Needing to Compensate If Children Are Learning Less

It would be unreasonable to expect student teachers to be as effective as their cooperating teachers in getting a lesson across. That's not to say that it isn't frustrating for you to recognize how much less your students may be learning, knowing that it is your responsibility to make up for it.

"I try to give a lot of leeway and try to feel comfortable letting student teachers do the lessons they want to do. One of my student teachers was working hard to do student-centered activities and have the kids evaluate themselves. But the process seemed to become more important than anything else, and she lost sight of her learning goals. She was working hard but she didn't realize things were falling apart around the edges and kids were doing lower quality work. It was frustrating to watch my kids do less than they were able to—and be rude to each other while doing it!" (COOPERATING TEACHER)

"For me, the pace of the curriculum can be frustrating. I have to set aside a couple of hours for a student teacher to do a lesson that might take me forty-five minutes—plus I often need to set aside time the next day for her to finish it." (COOPERATING TEACHER)

Deciding What to Do If Practices Conflict

The differences in how a student teacher works with your class can be a source of considerable tension for you. Sometimes the differences are those of style, and you may choose to hold your tongue and bide your time. At other times, however, you may feel that the students are suffering from the change in practice and decide to negotiate a return to a routine that works.

"I had a student teacher who had a really hard time allowing the students to do silent reading independently. Perhaps he didn't understand all the benefits of it and how it allows a teacher to observe students and note their progress as readers. Instead, he put kids on his lap and read aloud to them. He felt that it wasn't something they were getting at home—which was true—and they loved this opportunity to receive that special attention. But my goal during silent reading time is to see what the kids can do. Can they pick up a book, look at the front, go to the back? Can they turn the pages left to right? Are they tracking? Can they look at a book for a long time, or do they get ten books and not really look at them? So I gave my student teacher a clipboard and asked him to observe during silent reading time, to take notes about what he was seeing and what individual students were doing. I wanted to increase his skills as an observer and also to get him out of the pattern of reading to the children during that time." (COOPERATING TEACHER)

"My student teacher could tolerate a lot more noise than I ever could. At first when she was teaching I thought the kids were talking too loudly and out of turn, but the more I observed, the more I saw that they were engaged and on task. But the kids knew that with me it had to be quieter. Early on I let them know that even though the student teacher didn't mind lots of noise, for me to teach with so much noise hurts my ears and gives me a headache. It worked out all right because the bottom line was that the student teacher and I had the same goals, and she was very respectful that this was my classroom and knew that there were reasons why I did things certain ways." (COOPERATING TEACHER)

Needing to Intervene If Children Are Feeling Unsafe

It can be difficult to balance the student teacher's need to have authority in the classroom with obligations to provide a safe learning environment for the students. In general, the goal is to trust the student teacher to avoid situations that are hurtful or dangerous. At times, however, even though it can seriously undermine the student teacher's authority, it may become necessary for you to step in.

"The strain between us came, for me, late in the placement because I was really trusting the process. We seemed to be having good conversations, we had a great personal relationship, and things seemed to be moving down the right road. Then all of a sudden during the takeover what I saw happen in the classroom was not okay. I didn't feel equipped to do anything about it. I felt paralyzed by the fact that it was supposed to be her ten days—she was supposed to make it or break it—and if I stepped in, how would she ever know? But it had become an unsafe classroom. Chairs were being thrown and children were fighting. Everyone was suffering, including the student teacher. I realize now that if I ever have a student teacher who even *looks* like she's having that problem, then I have to intervene because of my commitment to the children. I can't put them in a place where they might not be safe." (COOPERATING TEACHER)

"One year I really sacrificed the kids. I felt so responsible for the student teacher's placement, and for letting her try things out, that I just didn't take care of the kids. I think a cooperating teacher has to say to the student teacher on day one, 'The kids come first.'" (COOPERATING TEACHER)

The professional edge you have in any relationship with a student teacher may not protect you from some unsettling personal reactions to having a student teacher who doesn't think you walk on water. Even more unsettling may be discovering that you are a little jealous of the student teacher's relationships with your students, or finding that you are avoiding treating your student teacher as honestly as might be good for him or her.

Feeling Judged

Cooperating teachers are not immune from feeling judged by their student teachers. Some of them have only to remember their own student teaching days!

> "I should pull out some of my journals from when I first started student teaching. Oh, the judgmental things I said about my cooperating teacher in my journal—and now I think she's one of the best teachers I ever worked with! But I remember coming in and thinking it looked like the military or something. It was fourth grade in a really tough school with a high number of poor and disenfranchised students, and I had strong ideas about what they needed. But all I had was my idealism to go on." (COOPERATING TEACHER)

> "My student teacher and I had very different beliefs, and I know she was always judging me. I got the feeling that she was saying to herself, 'I wouldn't do it that way. I wouldn't call out anyone's name. I wouldn't control so much.' I think she really trusted my love and connection with the children, but fundamentally she saw me as one of those well-intentioned, high-energy teachers who really don't know the needs of their children." (COOPERATING TEACHER)

Having Relationships with Children Change

Working with a student teacher can dilute or interfere with a teacher's relationships with students. Even though the student teacher needs to forge his or her own positive relationships with kids, the process can sometimes seem to diminish the strength of the teacher's own relationships with students.

Feeling the Responsibility to Give Honest, Constructive Feedback Even When It Might Be Hard for the Student Teacher to Hear

It can be difficult for you when the student teacher—who is often a helpful colleague—makes mistakes and requires lots of guidance, time, and corrective feedback. Sometimes it's hard for a cooperating teacher to even know where to start, and it's always a challenge to be honest yet supportive if things aren't going well.

"I had a student teacher who was picking up and holding the kindergart-
ners at inappropriate times. I'm quite affectionate with my kids, too. But
sometimes I would turn off the lights to signal clean-up time, and my student teacher would still be holding someone in her arms, or asking about
the play that had been happening. She was not helping me get the class
to the next activity. And I felt bad about not being able to draw the line.
When I turn the lights off, I expect my student teacher's assistance in
getting the class to the next place. It took me a long time to get what
I needed from her because I didn't want to be too direct. I talked more
about the kids and said things to the class like, 'Okay, we all need to be
helping now!' But I realize now that I should have spoken to her directly
about my goals for the classroom and how she could support them."
(COOPERATING TEACHER)

"Sometimes I'm observing a lesson and I notice that the academic level
has dropped and the kids are not together—they are writing too little,
talking too much, getting off task, and not being particularly nice to each
other. It's just obvious in these moments that the student teacher is not
holding high standards for any part of it. But where do you start? Some-
how it doesn't seem right simply to say, 'How did you like your lesson?'"
(COOPERATING TEACHER)

For all these reasons, it is crucial to lay the groundwork early on for a positive relationship—not only between the children and your student teacher, but between you and the
student teacher, as well. When it works, the process of mentoring a student teacher is
professionally fulfilling, of tremendous value to the student teacher, and probably the
strongest single influence on his or her practice.

The Benefits for the Student Teacher

Although student teachers know that you are changing your role in order to turn authority over to them, they may not really understand what it means for you to have your classroom become someone else's laboratory. The practical value to student teachers of having
that laboratory situation, and the professional value of having the support of someone
who can act as both a colleague and a mentor, are benefits that many student teachers
fully perceive only later in their careers.

Practical Help

- Having a laboratory for learning pedagogy
- Having a laboratory for learning classroom management
- Having someone to share the load

Professional Boost

- Having an accomplished mentor
- Having a supportive mentor
- Having a colleague in learning

In the laboratory that is your classroom, student teachers are able to observe your concrete teaching and classroom management strategies in action. They can also try out some of the things you model or some of their own ideas, and they can ask for help planning and managing any of it to the degree they feel unsure of themselves.

Having a Laboratory for Learning Pedagogy

Most student teachers have a lot to put together, not the least of which is helping children learn. With your guidance, a student teacher can learn specific ways to teach effectively, and also observe why certain practices are effective.

"During my lessons I made sure that I tried to set up things for students to do that were really hands-on and based on their interests and what they were needing at the time. It seemed that the more hands-on my lessons were, the better. It was during those lessons that I was trying most to model the same strategies that I would see my cooperating teacher using with the kids." (STUDENT TEACHER)

"My cooperating teacher urged me to familiarize myself with a book he was about to read aloud—not because of the particular book, he pointed out, but as a general rule to always read the book or try the activity before you ask your students to do something. I found this to be extremely important because not only was I better prepared to present the material and to anticipate any pitfalls, but it meant that I could relate to what kids were going through as they worked their way through the curriculum." (STUDENT TEACHER)

Having a Laboratory for Learning Classroom Management

Good classroom management can take a student teacher years to learn, but being in the classroom of a cooperating teacher who makes what he or she is doing transparent accelerates the process enormously. It also makes it easier for the student teacher to try some of those same strategies.

> "I learn the most when my cooperating teacher takes the time to explain, 'I'm doing this because the children need to know that I'm fair,' or 'I handled that situation in this way because these two children have a history of not getting along for partner work.' It's fascinating to get a behind-the-scenes look at what he's doing." (STUDENT TEACHER)

> "My cooperating teacher encouraged me to prepare students to work together before they got started on lessons. So every time I introduced an activity in which children would have to work together, I started with a class meeting and role-played with a student what it would look like, for example, to share math manipulatives. We role-played the trouble spots and then talked about how it felt and how we could do it differently. It worked well because the children came up with their own ideas about how to work together, and I was able to avoid just telling them I didn't want to see this or that happening." (STUDENT TEACHER)

> "Even though I had the same philosophy as my master teacher, it was fine-tuned when I was with her. She was living her philosophy; it was real. I learned about the day-to-day interactions, the day-to-day ways to relate to kids, the day-to-day ways she would help them think about how to be fair or how to work as a team—before anything would ever happen as well as when there was a problem. I learned to copy some of the things she would do, some of the ways I saw her work with kids and solve problems with them. I would try those too when I was teaching." (STUDENT TEACHER)

Having Someone to Share the Load

It's a comfort for student teachers to know that there is someone who can manage aspects of a lesson if help is needed or can manage a particular group of students if they begin to struggle.

"I had students doing partner interviews, but with just a twenty-minute period, only a few of the pairs were able to get started on their writing. This was particularly frustrating since it was a Thursday and I wouldn't be back until the following Tuesday, at which time I was sure that many groups would have forgotten what they had talked about. Luckily, my cooperating teacher and I had a few moments to reflect on the process at the end of the day, and he offered to follow up with the class the very next day." (STUDENT TEACHER)

In addition to the practical help you offer a student teacher, you provide a professional boost with almost everything you do—as a mentor and colleague.

Having an Accomplished Mentor

The relationship between a student teacher and a cooperating teacher is a unique apprenticeship opportunity—a chance for the student teacher to learn directly from a more accomplished fellow professional who is invested in his or her success.

"I walked into my placement and takeover armed with this philosophy [constructivism]. I walked out exhausted—but ever-more determined to align my practice with my ideals. If there was one thing I learned, it was that democratic, student-centered classrooms are an attainable and vital goal. With the help of my master teacher I rigorously analyzed each and every aspect of my practice: my interaction with students, my questioning techniques, my lesson plans, my curricular decisions, etcetera. In many instances, my practice fell far short of the ideals I had set for myself. My faith in those ideals, however, was never shaken." (STUDENT TEACHER)

"I really learned about classroom respect from watching my cooperating teacher interact with her kids. She always gave her students respect. She made her classroom a real bright spot, and I could see the kids were the better for it. She had faith in them and believed they could all succeed. She would say to them, 'This is your chance. You're a sharp kid and you can do this.' From the kids' conversations you could tell that they took what was going on in the classroom back into their home lives and neighborhoods and made better decisions because of what they learned in her class." (STUDENT TEACHER)

Having a Supportive Mentor

Sometimes the most important role cooperating teachers play is that of offering friendship and support. Student teachers feel lucky to have such relationships as they make their vulnerable way through their first real teaching experiences.

> "I felt completely safe to make mistakes and then to have to backtrack and figure out what to do about it. My cooperating teacher was willing to let me try new things and stayed very accepting and nonjudgmental throughout the whole process." (STUDENT TEACHER)

> "She is an amazing communicator. Right away I knew that this was a person who would be a friend as well as a professional ally." (STUDENT TEACHER)

Having a Colleague in Learning

In addition to being a mentor, a cooperating teacher can be a true colleague who is learning along with the student teacher. In this kind of relationship, the cooperating teacher mentors not only the student teacher's classroom skills, but also his or her skills at becoming a collegial learning partner.

> "Witnessing my master teacher's class meeting began to answer some of the questions I had about this type of meeting, but at the same time it raised many more. My master teacher and I have begun to talk in depth about *las reuniónes de la clase* because neither of us have had much prior experience with them. She is doing the best she knows and is very open to suggestions and information. I am looking forward to working with her to explore class meetings and their possibilities for our classroom." (STUDENT TEACHER)

The Challenges for the Student Teacher

Student teachers' fledgling professional ideas and their personal self-confidence can be put to the test in the inherently unequal relationships between student teachers and cooperating teachers. Student teachers can easily feel professionally and personally vulnerable in their relationship with you.

Professional Challenges

- Being a guest in someone else's classroom
- Deciding what to do if practices conflict
- Having authority undermined

Personal Challenges

- Believing that one's ideas are being dismissed
- Dealing with rivalries
- Asking for and getting honest, useful feedback

Just as cooperating teachers experience the strains of being full-time hosts, student teachers struggle with their status as guests. In some situations, they may even find their professionalism undermined.

Being a Guest in Someone Else's Classroom

A student teacher can experience as awkward or even disconcerting the limitations that arise from being a visitor or temporary resident in a cooperating teacher's room.

> "I think the hardest part about being a student teacher was feeling the need to do what the teacher wanted—and doing it the way she wanted it done. It was her classroom and I didn't want to make it tough for either of us, or the kids, for that matter!" (STUDENT TEACHER)

> "It was frustrating trying to lead class meetings and instructional conversations about literature selections in a placement where not much time had been spent to create a sense of deep community. Although my master teacher was very concerned with and cared deeply about her students, she hadn't really approached moral development in a very structured manner. So, even though she was receptive to my doing these activities, they just ended up being kind of plopped down out of nowhere." (STUDENT TEACHER)

Deciding What to Do If Practices Conflict

Conflicts over teaching practices can be stumbling blocks for student teachers regardless of the significance of a particular practice. Only sometimes are they able to handle such differences gracefully.

"My cooperating teacher was more focused on extrinsic rewards and pun-ishments than I was. And what came out of the children's mouths when I started my takeover was, 'You don't give out as many points as she does!' So I had to work with the kids to help them understand they could still count on me to be kind and fair, even though I didn't give out points." (STUDENT TEACHER)

"I believe children can benefit from the opportunity to draw pictures while they hear a story read aloud, but I know my cooperating teacher doesn't like the idea. He actually told me it is not something he does and that he's seen it in other classrooms and doesn't think it's an effective strat-egy. However, when I had my takeover I decided to let my kids draw while I read, even though I knew my cooperating teacher wouldn't value it." (STUDENT TEACHER)

Having Authority Undermined

A cooperating teacher has enormous power in how the student teacher and children view the student teacher's authority in the classroom. Sometimes messages about authority are communicated structurally, by limiting the student teacher's role. In other cases, a coop-erating teacher may intervene inappropriately or in a way that undermines the student teacher.

"My cooperating teacher never gave me the impression that I was invited to take on real responsibility in the classroom. She basically introduced me to the class and said, 'She's going to be with us for the rest of the semester and she's going to help me here and there.' I worked independently with a reading group, and that was meaningful, but nothing was really open for me. I would always have to ask, 'Is it okay if I do this? Is it okay if I do that?' I never felt comfortable taking any initiative." (STUDENT TEACHER)

"When I was teaching and my cooperating teacher felt that the room was getting too noisy, he just stepped in and told the children to be quiet. But I was usually fine with the noise level and had already given kids the message that the noise level was okay." (STUDENT TEACHER)

In some instances, a student teacher may need to draw on personal reserves of character to deal with feelings of not being fairly treated by the cooperating teacher.

Believing That One's Ideas Are Being Dismissed

Knowing that a cooperating teacher does not value one's ideas is at best discouraging for a student teacher. At worst, it sometimes means the student teacher is powerless to carry out his or her plans.

"Sometimes I wanted to try something and I could tell that my cooperating teacher didn't think it was a good idea. He would say, 'Well, you can try it once,' which usually had the effect of my not trying it at all." (STUDENT TEACHER)

"I found that with partner work, a few groups worked beautifully together, but many others did not. I was spending a lot of my time trying to get students to focus on the activity. I decided that the children needed more explicit instruction about how to work well with partners. Although my cooperating teacher agreed that the students were having trouble, he concluded that they simply couldn't work well in partnerships and decided to limit such activities because they were 'too exhausting' for him and 'too disruptive' to the flow of the school day." (STUDENT TEACHER)

Dealing with Rivalries

Whether working to build relationships with children or seeking acknowledgement for a classroom project, a student teacher can find him- or herself competing with the cooperating teacher in a way that feels confusing.

"I hit it off really well with the kids when I first got there, and within a few weeks they started talking to me and asking me questions more than they did the cooperating teacher. I think it might have hurt his feelings. To complicate matters, he went out on sick leave for a few weeks and when he came back it really seemed to bother him that I was more like their real teacher." (STUDENT TEACHER)

"When I was a student teacher, I came up with a lesson that engaged children in writing letters to the victims of a fire in a neighboring community. The letters were picked up by a local television station, and the radio station called as well. The whole thing was big and exciting for the kids. And my cooperating teacher, who was wonderful in many ways, really hurt me by taking over whenever something exciting happened—he took the kids on the trip to the radio station, and when the TV crew came to interview the class, he participated and I was not really included." (COOPERATING TEACHER)

Asking for and Getting Honest, Useful Feedback

Not all cooperating teachers feel comfortable giving critical feedback, so they may only talk about what student teachers did well. For student teachers who feel they aren't getting enough constructive advice, it can be a challenge to figure out how to ask for and get honest feedback.

> "I wanted more direction from my cooperating teacher. Sometimes he seemed to be so overwhelmed by my questions that he'd just say, 'You need to figure it out for yourself.' He seemed to think I was looking to him to tell me exactly what to do, but what I really needed was more help and guidance." (STUDENT TEACHER)

> "I created my own lesson plans but always asked my cooperating teacher to look them over with me in advance. I'd write up my ideas or talk them through with her and she would ask questions, identify potential trouble spots, and point me toward resources and material to look over for ideas. Then I'd revise and show them to her again. Not only did I learn about putting plans together through this process, but it really felt as though we were co-teachers." (STUDENT TEACHER)

It may seem a bit ungracious to end this chapter with so many complaints from the very colleagues you are trying to help, but student teachers have few opportunities to let you in on their particular struggles with cooperating teachers. While you have a professional obligation to let them know what they could improve or should avoid, they rarely feel able to reciprocate.

3

Getting Started
as Colleagues

F YOUR CLASSROOM FEELS WELCOMING TO THE STUDENT TEACHER, it will be a lot easier for him or her to understand why a feeling of community is important to you as the master teacher—as well as how you achieve it. On the other hand, you both will pay a big price if you skip the initial steps of helping your student teacher get comfortable and prepared for joining your class.

> "My cooperating teacher never sat down with me to talk about goals or expectations. By the time we tried to do this it was too late—our relationship had deteriorated. He wasn't sure where I was going, I felt unsupported, and he didn't know how to help me." (STUDENT TEACHER)

Laying the Groundwork: Your First Meetings

Cooperating teachers and student teachers alike say there's nothing worse than finding themselves—practically strangers—matched up and in front of the children before having had any time to get to know one another or share goals and expectations for the student-teaching experience. Ideally, a student teacher will have had a chance to observe your classroom for a few days before it is decided that the two of you are a good match.

Once you are matched, it is critical to take some time for initial getting-to-know-you conversations. Whether they are structured meetings or informal chats, these conversations not only help ward off future problems, but also can build a base for ongoing communication and learning from one another. In these first meetings, you can make it clear from the start that you are there to help the student teacher and that you are also committed to building a two-way learning relationship.

> "The very first time I met her, I had a strong sense of my cooperating teacher. Right away she told me, 'You know, I'm the type of person who says exactly what's on my mind, and sometimes people have a really hard time with that. But I want you to know, right up front, this is how I've always been. I'm going to tell you things that I feel or things that I see, and I hope that you could do that with me.'" (STUDENT TEACHER)

No matter what topics you discuss in your first meetings, these encounters are an important time for each of you to communicate something of who you are as people. They give you a chance to converse informally, letting the two of you begin to learn about and develop empathy for each other as unique individuals. Initial meetings are also an important time for you to provide the student teacher with background information about the school and the children; to talk about your goals for the classroom, your style, and your general philosophy about teaching and class management; and to set out clear expectations for how you will work together.

Giving Background Information

Often a cooperating teacher will start a first meeting by describing how he or she decided to become a teacher, or what his or her own student teaching experience was like, or how teaching seems to extend into his or her family life. In this way, by communicating your interest in establishing a friendly relationship, you make it easier for the student teacher to volunteer personal information, and to approach you with questions or concerns in the future.

In a first meeting your student teacher is likely to want to know about the school itself—the underlying philosophy about children, teaching, and learning; how the faculty interacts; and what kind of parent involvement to expect. But of even more interest will be what you can describe about the progress of individual children and the class as a whole and what you are working on academically, socially, and ethically.

Sharing Goals and Philosophies

As you discuss your students, it will be important that your student teacher learn as much as possible about your educational goals and philosophy. What academic goals and expectations do you have for students? What social goals are you working toward? Try to describe your philosophy, what you believe about children and their development, and how this plays out in day-to-day life in your classroom. Describe some of the ways you manage the classroom and help children take responsibility for both their learning and their behavior.

Encourage your student teacher to respond by sharing his or her own philosophy, ideas about the kind of teacher he or she wants to be, and goals for the classroom and the children. Take some time to learn about his or her hopes for student teaching as a learning experience.

It is important, too, to understand the philosophy and goals of your student teacher's university program. In addition to what you learn from him or her, try to find out more through your student teacher's university-based supervisor or an orientation or credit course offered by the university. It is likely that the better you understand your student teacher's university program, the better you will understand his or her teaching goals and decisions—and the better the alliance will be that the two of you forge in the classroom.

Discussing Expectations and Logistics

It is common for student teachers to have at least two student-teaching experiences—an introductory teaching experience when they are in the classroom only part-time; and then a practicum when they are in the classroom every day, take on more responsibility over time, and plan and execute a culminating "takeover." Every teacher education program is different, so it's important to understand a university's expectations for its students and to talk with your student teacher about how those expectations translate into the relative amounts of observing, assisting, and teaching he or she will actually do.

In addition to having clear expectations about how much of each kind of activity the student teacher will perform, it will be especially important to talk about each of your roles during each kind of activity. When the student teacher is an observer, where will he or she actually be stationed, or will he or she be moving around the room? In what situations will you expect the student teacher to be an assistant rather than primarily an observer? Are there general guidelines for how you want the student teacher to assist, or will you give specific directions in each situation? When the student teacher is teaching, what are his or her expectations about your role? Will you be a co-teacher or an observer? Discuss the issue of intervention and what you are both comfortable with. When, if at all, would you step in? How would you do it? How can he or she ask for help on the spot? You will also want to agree on a way to debrief each other on the day's experiences and to get a sense of how much you each expect to participate in the other's curriculum planning. These are the big issues, but don't overlook the student teacher's need for a home base in your room. Will you provide a desk, a table, a special corner? Where can the student teacher store things or hang a hat? As in dealing with the kids on the first day of school, it's wise to dispense with logistics before they become anxieties.

Again, every practicum is different, and every student teacher-cooperating teacher pair is uniquely individual. You are the best person to judge your situation and decide what topics are most important to focus on. Consider the list in "Tool 1: First Meetings" as flexible and suggestive rather than prescriptive. It may be that these ideas help you structure your early conversations with your student teacher; alternatively, together you may prefer to create your own list of topics to discuss.

> "My cooperating teacher wanted to set up a meeting with me even before my placement started so that I could ask her questions and we could get acquainted. That meeting really set the stage for the entire experience. Now I spend thirty to forty-five minutes with her before or after school regularly. I go over what I feel are my strengths and weaknesses, what I can

plan for the upcoming week, and how I feel about the school. It's wonderful for me to have someone so involved in what I'm doing!" (STUDENT TEACHER)

Welcoming the Student Teacher into the Community

"I made a mistake when I introduced my student teacher to the kids. I told the class that she was an 'expert' from the university and that she was coming to help teach and see how children learn and all that kind of stuff. I guess I was trying to set it up so that she would be equally respected. Well, during the first few lessons it was obvious that her management skills were not the skills of an expert. So I called a class meeting, and I asked the kids to think about a time when they did something for the very first time. They talked about learning to ride a bike or read, and I said, 'You know, Ms. Lawrence has been taking all of these classes at the university about how to teach, and in a way she's an expert in learning about kids and how to teach lessons, but now she's come in to try teaching for the very first time. So what can we do to help?' The kids were very sweet and said things like, 'We need to not talk when she's teaching,' and so on. It gave them a chance to see the situation for what it was—and to be helpful."
(COOPERATING TEACHER)

The importance of making the student teacher feel welcome goes without saying. You play a vital role in helping the children see the student teacher as your friend and colleague and as someone who deserves their full respect and attention. It will make your student teacher's day (and entire semester) if you are able to engage the children in welcoming the student teacher in meaningful ways, individually and as a community. And be sure to let the student teacher plan a welcome of his or her own—a special way of introducing him- or herself to the class.

"One of the best things that my student teacher did was the way she introduced herself to the kids. She created a poster about herself and showed the children pictures of what was important to her—'This is my husband. This is my dog and my cat.' And my kids just loved it. They ask about the cat all the time. It's given them a connection with who she is and how she lives."
(COOPERATING TEACHER)

TOOL 1 First Meetings

BACKGROUND INFORMATION

Share some personal background

▶ How did you each choose teaching and what have your experiences been?

▶ What is the student teacher experiencing in her teacher preparation program?

Tell the student teacher informally about the school

▶ Describe the school mission and its philosophy, leadership, teachers, students, families, and community.

▶ Describe individual children and the class as a whole.

▶ What has happened so far?

▶ Where are the children academically, socially, and ethically?

▶ What has been challenging?

▶ What has gone well?

▶ What's next?

GOALS AND PHILOSOPHY

Share your goals for the classroom

▶ What are you trying to accomplish this year?

▶ In what ways are you trying to help children develop?

▶ Ask the student teacher to share his own goals for the classroom and what he understands to be the goals of his teacher preparation program.

▶ Discuss how your views might be similar to and/or different from each other's.

Talk about social and ethical development

▶ How do moral issues play a role in the classroom?

▶ What kind of learning community are you trying to create?

▶ Find out more about your student teacher's perspective.

Talk about classroom management

▶ Explain your approach to classroom management and discipline.

▶ How did you create norms for behavior, and what are they?

▶ How do you help students take responsibility for their behavior and learning? What do you do to help students learn to resolve conflicts?

▶ Ask the student teacher to share his reactions, views, and expectations with regard to classroom management.

▶ Ask the student teacher what his teacher preparation program teaches about classroom management.

Talk about curriculum

▶ Talk about content and how you approach it in your curriculum.

▶ What concepts, skills, and strategies are you trying to teach children?

First Meetings TOOL1

▶ Ask the student teacher to talk about special interests related to curriculum, and what he might want to focus on during his practicum.

▶ Ask the student teacher to explain the expectations and requirements of his teacher education program as they relate to curriculum.

EXPECTATIONS AND LOGISTICS

Clarify the student teacher's expectations

▶ Ask the student teacher what she would like to take on during her time in your classroom.

▶ What do observing and assisting mean to each of you?

▶ How much is she hoping to teach or co-teach?

▶ What is her schedule going to be?

Share your thoughts about your role

▶ Will you observe and offer feedback?

▶ Will you co-teach?

▶ How will you hand off increasing responsibility?

Plan for planning and debriefing

▶ Share ideas about how each of you would like to handle planning and debriefing.

Plan an introduction to the kids and their families

▶ Talk about your plans for introducing the student teacher to the class.

▶ Describe how you might introduce her to parents.

▶ Encourage her to come up with her own ways of introducing herself to both.

Talk about coats, books, and bodies

▶ Make sure your student teacher has a home base and a place for her things.

▶ Talk about where she will be while you are teaching.

▶ Talk about where you will be while she is teaching.

Reiterate "we're in this together"

▶ Be sure you've been clear about the things that are really important to you.

▶ Be sure you've communicated that you are open to learning a lot from her.

▶ Be sure she's had a chance to talk about what she's looking forward to.

▶ Invite her to talk about anything she is feeling concerned about.

TOOL2 Welcome

▶ Put the student teacher's name on the classroom door with yours and set up a desk or create a special space for him.

▶ Engage students in preparing a written guide to your classroom.

▶ Ask the children to write individual welcome notes about themselves.

▶ Have a community circle meeting to introduce and welcome the student teacher, and have students describe class norms.

▶ Encourage the student teacher to introduce himself to the class in an engaging way.

▶ Invite the student teacher to create a "special person" display.

▶ Invite volunteers to take the student teacher on a tour of the school.

▶ Consistently say "Mr. [STUDENT TEACHER] and I" when talking to the class.

▶ Co-teach with the student teacher, especially early on.

▶ Introduce the student teacher to other staff members and the principal.

▶ Arrange for the student teacher to observe in other teachers' classrooms.

Some cooperating teachers say that letting a student teacher into the tight-knit circle of relationships in the classroom can be hard, and that not just one or two but a number of self-conscious efforts such as those described in "Tool 2: Welcome" are important—especially if it is the middle of the school year. A warm welcome also serves as the first step in building the reserve of trust that you all may need farther down the line. With all the stumbling that lies ahead for the student teacher, the more you are able to integrate him or her into the classroom community, the more likely he or she is to experience a buffer of good will when it's most needed.

Exchanging Information about the Children

One of the most effective ways to integrate your student teacher into the classroom is to spend time exchanging information about what you are each learning about the children in your class. In contrast to the potentially more difficult time you spend analyzing teaching performances—both of yours—sharing information and observations about students allows you to appreciate your common delight in the children in your care and your concern for them as well.

Information Exchange TOOL3

FORMAL STRUCTURES TO TRY

▶ Have the student teacher keep a notebook tracking the strengths and weaknesses of each child or a subgroup of children. Also have the student teacher make notes about the ways to deal with these strengths and weaknesses. Periodically review these observations together and decide how to respond to the children.

▶ From time to time, ask the student teacher to observe closely and record the behavior of a child or small group that is having difficulty. Together develop ways to better meet each child's needs.

▶ Choose a child (or at most two) that you both focus on for a day. Try to observe the day through the eyes of the child. Debrief your observations at the end of the day, drawing on immediate observations and past interactions with the child.

▶ Each of you observe different children, but with the same focusing question—for example, How is the child building autonomy? or How does the child collaborate with others? Share your observations and their implications for how to work with these children.

PRINCIPLES FOR LEARNING MORE

▶ Model and explain the importance of making a special effort to develop friendly relationships with the children who exhibit the most frustrating behavior, since the typical and least effective response is to ignore such children when possible.

▶ Share relevant information about children's families with the student teacher so that she can understand the children better.

▶ Ask your student teacher to apply the principles of her teacher education program to what she is noticing in your classroom about children's development—academically, socially, ethically, and motivationally.

"You may be focusing on working with a particular child, and then, all of a sudden there's a huge surprise with some other child. It's like, 'Look at this other one over here, this daffodil in the corner. Blossoming!' And you can talk it over with your student teacher—what seems to be working?" (COOPERATING TEACHER)

In your two-way conversations about the children, the student teacher needs to tap into your insights about the children, and you can also elicit the student teacher's help in gathering new information. At the same time that your student teacher is building his or her independent experiences of the children, he or she can be helping you learn more: How is Darrell managing partner work? Is Alicia making progress standing up for herself? What seems to trigger Ming's inappropriate behavior? Is each student's need to feel competent being met? What circumstances in the class are detracting from a sense of community?

The goal is to develop an ongoing, open-ended conversation about the children and their growth as you meet formally and informally throughout the practicum. It's a wonderful benefit of having two unique, caring adults in the room!

"I tell my student teacher some background about the children and their families. I think it makes sense, for example, when a child comes back from a weekend visiting his father—who is living in a car—to explain, 'Ryan often has a hard time on Mondays because his father is homeless right now.' Then if she needs to put Ryan on time out, she can make a connection with him—something like, 'Hey, I know you had a hard weekend, and I know this lesson was hard, but I had to put you on time out because you were interfering with other people's learning.' This way the student teacher has information that lets her acknowledge where the child is coming from." (COOPERATING TEACHER)

"My cooperating teacher tells me almost everything she's thinking about as she's teaching. And if a child has a problem, she'll let me into the nuances that I can observe for—nuances that I need to know as a teacher." (STUDENT TEACHER)

"We would spend time during our breaks talking about the kids, and my cooperating teacher would say things like, 'This is how his personal life is right now,' or 'These are some things I've noticed about this child,' or 'This is what she seems to be good at.' It also helped me understand the kids when after class my cooperating teacher would sit down and say, 'This is what happened. This is the reason I felt it was important to do this with this child.' It helped me a lot because everything was so situational. Her methods were pretty much the same along the lines of showing mutual respect and such, but different strategies worked best with different kids and different situations." (STUDENT TEACHER)

In addition to the informal observations of students that fill each day in a classroom, you and your student teacher may want to incorporate some of the suggestions in "Tool 3: Information Exchange." Plan ways to collect data and debrief each other on what you are learning, and be sure your student teacher understands the importance of learning about the least appealing or most frustrating children as well as those with whom he or she has an easy relationship.

Finally, take time to talk about any connections your student teacher is making between what he or she sees happening in the classroom and what he or she is studying in the university teacher education program. Such discussions help the student teacher consolidate what he or she is learning, give you more information about the university program that is shaping his or her perceptions and teaching decisions, and may also help you think about your classroom in new ways.

4

Coaching
Issues

IN THE RELATIONSHIP BETWEEN YOU AND YOUR STUDENT TEACHER, THE TENSION between being colleagues and exchanging feedback about one another's practice is real, and it's an important reason for you to establish a friendly, collegial relationship as soon as possible—and to keep working at it. Honest, constructive feedback is easier to hear from someone who we trust has our best interests at heart.

Although the term *coaching* is usually thought of as observing and providing feedback, your role as a coach really begins indirectly, two steps before you give your student teacher feedback on his or her practice. First of all in the coaching process, you are a model. Your student teacher is constantly aware of what you do in the classroom, so you are always teaching by example. The second step in the coaching that you do with your student teacher is to discuss *your* practice—not his or hers. The tone you set in conversation about your own practice—describing your purpose, acknowledging things you might have done differently, inviting the student teacher to question why you did something a particular way—sets the stage for the third step in the process: the direct coaching you perform when you debrief the student teacher's practice. In this third step, your role includes both informal conversations about "something I noticed" and formal, scheduled observations, with set times to debrief them.

When the Student Teacher Observes You

Your student teacher is always observing you to see how you manage the class, the curriculum, trouble spots, interruptions, and everything in between. On a practical level, you are constantly modeling how one teacher (you) goes about creating community and balancing the needs of the group with the needs of the individual, the need for control with the need for student autonomy, the need to support children's self-confidence with the need to challenge them to achieve at higher levels, and so forth. At times, what you do can feel so natural and automatic to you and look so effortless to the student teacher, that what's hard is breaking it down and helping the student teacher see all the pieces in what you achieve with the students.

> "I've had cooperating teachers who say, 'Okay, you should watch me and then you'll see what I do,' but there are so many different steps going on that it's just impossible to see it all." (STUDENT TEACHER)

When You Are Observed TOOL4

OBSERVATIONS

▶ Choose situations carefully to maximize student teacher's learning.

▶ Share your goals with the student teacher in advance.

▶ Urge the student teacher to take notes. You'll both forget!

▶ Sometimes focus your student teacher's observations on specific aspects of the teaching day—the morning meeting and transition to the first curriculum activity, the reading and discussion of a story, and so on.

▶ Sometimes focus your student teacher's observations on a few children and have him "track" these children's experience with the lesson.

DEBRIEFING TOGETHER

▶ Encourage the student teacher to revisit your specific goals to see how they played out.

▶ Invite the student teacher to tell you what he saw and ask you questions about why you did what you did.

▶ If things did not go well (it happens to the best of us), this might be an opportunity to ask the student teacher for any suggestions for the future.

▶ If the student teacher misses things that you did that you think are important, point these out.

▶ Perhaps the student teacher would have done something quite different from what you did—what might she have tried, and why?

▶ Write down the things you are learning from each other. You'll both forget!

▶ Help your student teacher make arrangements to observe other classrooms in the school to gain exposure to a variety of teaching styles and approaches.

"He was very aware of what he called 'the layers of teaching' that student
teachers need to learn to be responsible for." (STUDENT TEACHER)

As the student teacher observes your lessons and management style, his or her recorded
noticings and questions can serve as the fodder for a rich discussion. The more you can
use observation and discussion techniques to "unpack" what you did, what went well,
what was challenging, and what you might have done instead (or next time), the more
you both will learn from one another.

Another advantage for the student teacher of taking detailed observation notes is that
besides providing a list of concrete, specific things to talk over with you, it will also give
your student teacher some concrete, specific techniques to review and try out later.

> "There were times when I would just sit in the discussion circle and liter-
> ally transcribe everything students said and how my cooperating teacher
> responded. I had pages of dialogue. I couldn't believe how fast I could
> write! Each night I could pore over these notes and study his responses—
> how he would stay neutral as a facilitator, draw kids out, stay fair, and
> handle distractions of all kinds. I learned to say things [to the students in
> class] like, 'That's an interesting opinion, do you have any evidence to back
> it up?' or 'Who has something to add to that?' It was a great way to learn."
> (STUDENT TEACHER)

Sometimes when the student teacher observes you, he or she may have questions, suggestions, or ideas to share about what he or she might have done differently. These can
be hard discussions to have—especially when your student teacher's ideas are quite different from yours. Such discussions are well worth having, but they require that both of
you make a strong effort to hear what the other person is saying and to understand the
situation as the other person sees it. These exchanges may actually reveal important similarities in your goals and beliefs about teaching. And when they reveal important differences, they have great potential to increase your ability to help the student teacher grow—
and to grow yourself.

> "I modeled a math activity for my children to do individually, using scales.
> They all said they understood, but when they got into the activity there
> was utter chaos! Later my student teacher agreed that the kids were having
> a hard time and said, 'I think it was too complicated and you were asking
> them to do too many things on the worksheet.' She suggested folding the
> sheet in half and having partners work together to answer the questions.
> And so I told her, 'Watch me this afternoon when I do this again, because

When You Observe TOOL5

OBSERVATIONS

▶ Choose situations carefully to maximize student teacher's learning.

▶ Ask the student teacher in advance about his broad or specific goals, or ask if there's anything particular he would like you to look for.

▶ Take notes. You'll both forget!

▶ When possible, map your observations onto his goals for the day or activity.

▶ Sometimes focus your observations on specific aspects of the teaching day.

▶ Sometimes focus your observations on specific aspects of his practice— how he gives directions, gets children to shift from one activity to the next, facilitates discussion, and so on.

DEBRIEFING

▶ Ask the student teacher about her goals and how she's feeling about the way things went. What went well? What was challenging?

▶ Tell the student teacher what you saw and ask questions about why she chose to do things one way or another.

▶ Ask the student teacher what she thinks she could have done or might do differently next time.

▶ Share your own suggestions for next time with the student teacher.

▶ Urge her to take notes about anything she hopes to remember!

modifying lessons is something you're going to find yourself doing—and it's okay to do that.' After lunch I did the activity again, this time in partnerships, as she suggested, and it was much better. It was helpful to me and good for her to see her ideas implemented. She saw that I respected her advice and that it was okay for a teacher to change directions and admit to the kids that she's not perfect." (COOPERATING TEACHER)

When You Observe the Student Teacher

Observing and coaching the student teacher are two of the primary roles of being a cooperating teacher. As your student teacher takes on responsibility in the classroom, you are always watching what he or she does, what is working well, and where he or she needs guidance. In response to your student teacher's efforts, you are always trying to accompany your critique with professional support and personal caring.

> "When she observed my teaching, my cooperating teacher would always offer feedback in a very positive way, even when it was critical. I never felt that what she said was threatening to me personally." (STUDENT TEACHER)

> "I always felt this person was giving me really good feedback on my teaching as she saw it, and how it fit into her vision. She always made time to sit down and plan and talk together. We would do that by squeezing in a half hour or so every day. And many times we'd talk in the evening—about school, the classroom, my schooling, life." (STUDENT TEACHER)

Informally, you are aware of almost everything the student teacher does, and you provide supportive guidance and suggestions along the way. But when a student teacher does a formal lesson or activity or a full-day takeover, it makes sense to be deliberate and organized about observing and giving feedback. The more you can develop a regular process with your student teacher for observing and giving feedback, the more he or she will know what to expect and the easier it will be for both of you to reflect together and give honest feedback.

> "I always try to sit down with the student teacher before a lesson and ask what he or she hopes to accomplish. Then after observing, I like to get the student teacher's goals back on the table before I give feedback or make suggestions. I try to acknowledge that this is hard stuff to do and that there's a lot to think about. If I need to say, 'What do you think you could do next time?' I don't want it to be taken as criticism." (COOPERATING TEACHER)

The Whole Question of Intervening

Most cooperating teachers struggle with the issue of when and how to intervene. It can be hard to contain the impulse to jump in when the student teacher is trying to teach and things are going awry. The first challenge is to weigh the effect of doing so on the student teacher's confidence and relationship with the students against the damage or potential damage likely to befall the students if you don't intervene. The second challenge, if you decide it is necessary to intervene, is to do so in a way that continues to support (rather than undermine) the student teacher. You and your student teacher will want to have some clear guidelines about what circumstances could lead you to intervene and how you will do it—what you will say to the students and how you will communicate to the student teacher about it, either before or after the fact.

Not All Interventions Are for the Best

From a student teacher's perspective, some interventions are just wrong. The cooperating teacher may not have enough information to make a good decision about intervening. Nevertheless, once the cooperating teacher intervenes and asserts his or her authority, the dynamic of who's in charge changes, and the students and student teacher are left with little choice but to comply.

> "On Tuesday I was working with my reading group. We began by reviewing the agreements we had made last Thursday about how we wanted to behave and treat one another. I told them that I was impressed with their improvement but that I knew that this week we could manage to follow the guidelines even better. Unfortunately, David wasn't able to settle down as quickly as the rest of the group, but I was feeling confident that he was just about to, when suddenly the cooperating teacher called across the room for him to leave our group. I was frustrated and dismayed, but I also felt unable to go against her directive. And I'm sure that David was on the way to handling himself appropriately that day." (STUDENT TEACHER)

Sometimes, even when the cooperating teacher thinks he or she is helping the student teacher as unobtrusively as possible, the very act of intervening is undermining of the student teacher. Because the student teacher's sense of authority with the children is likely to be fragile, even a seemingly insignificant intervention can be devastating. No matter what your intention, if you take over or reassert yourself as the "more effective" authority, that's the message the students will pick up on.

> "When my student teacher was teaching, I would sit at my computer and give kids 'looks' and hand motions from the sidelines—all in an attempt to help maintain order. One day my student teacher told me after school that he'd prefer if I would call him over and tell him about the problem, rather than intervening with the kids directly. It really spoke to me and after that I held back. But on the other hand, you can't let it get to the point where things are unsafe, or the kids are blatantly in front of you throwing balls at the ceiling, and you just sit there typing away at your computer."
> (COOPERATING TEACHER)

Intervening in Ways That Do Not Undermine the Student Teacher

Whether to "just sit there" is the cooperating teacher's ultimate dilemma. Sometimes it *is* possible to act in the moment to achieve a win–win solution. You help, no one is undermined, and later you can talk over what you did with your student teacher.

> "My student teacher had developed two math centers on her own. She was in the middle of teaching the lesson and children at one center had finished the work and were just sitting there not knowing what to do. I automatically grabbed a tub of manipulatives and gave it to them along with an extension to work on. The supervisor from the teacher education program happened to be visiting that day and said, 'It was really important what you did, but that's the kind of thing you need to make the student teacher aware of, because she didn't realize what was happening.' And so I was able to talk with her about it. I think my student teacher needed to hear, too, that it was okay to step outside the original lesson plan and change or add to the lesson to meet kids' needs." (COOPERATING TEACHER)

Communicating with your student teacher about any intervention on your part not only helps him or her learn from the situation but also is essential to maintaining a collegial relationship. There may even be times when you want to communicate with your students as well as your student teacher about why you are intervening.

> "I had just made tremendous progress with one of my most challenging students, a girl who frequently yells out, interrupts my teaching, and corrects other students—behavior that is just unacceptable. I know in her heart April wants to do better, but she just can't always control herself. So I was thrilled when she came up with her own plan. When she interrupts my teaching, I'm supposed to give her a signal, and if she does it again, I need to ask her to think about and write down what it is she's doing that stops the learning. And if she still doesn't stop and I need to send her out of the room, I agreed to make a folder of work for her to do while she is out. We also agreed that when she finished the work, she could return and she would tell me what she thinks she did wrong. So we came up with this great agreement and we were both committed to getting her on track.
>
> The very next day, she got into an argument with her partner, Briana. They were working on a poster to display what they had learned in their research. Apparently April didn't like what Briana had written on the

poster and she scribbled all over it. My student teacher, seeing this as unacceptable behavior, which it was, told April that she needed to leave the room to think about what she had done. April started crying and apologizing and saying how she would 'undo' the damage she'd done to Briana's work. But the student teacher insisted that she leave the room, and I felt that my agreement with April to give her a signal and a chance to change before sending her out was being violated.

So I had to intervene. I called April and the student teacher over and said, 'Guys, let's think about this for a minute. April, you're thinking the student teacher is asking you to take time to think about things, and you sound ready to talk about it now and make it up to Briana.' She said yes, so I said, 'Why don't you and Briana go out in the hall and talk it out.' April and Briana both agreed and went off to talk. I also made sure that my student teacher understood exactly what I was working on with April and why. I feel a little bad about intervening like that, but I just felt that in that situation, my first responsibility was to April." (COOPERATING TEACHER)

Your Students Are Watching!

And no matter how considered your intervention, don't be surprised if students have some advice for you. One second-grade student wrote this letter to her teacher after he stepped in to "help" run the class during the student teacher's lesson:

Dear Mr. Henriquez,

I think Ms. Dana [the student teacher] should know by now how to run her class. I think she has lessened to you enuff to know what to do when some body is not lissening or is playing with some one els. I now that I should not be getting smart with a teacher. And I am sarry about that. But she should use her own thoughts. Next time would you let her do and think her own thinks and ideas? That would help her too when you are not in the class so she can learn that. Your sweet angle,

Love,

Erica

5

Your Role in Developing Student Teacher Understanding and Competencies

IF WE ASSUME THAT A STUDENT TEACHER IS TRYING TO DEVELOP A CARING
learning community—a safe place where children practice shared values (such
as respect, kindness, fairness, and responsibility) and are engaged in meaningful
and relevant learning experiences—then it is likely that the student teacher is striving
to build understanding and develop competency in at least four important areas:

- building relationships with students and families,
- establishing authority and control of the classroom,
- making values clear and consistent, and
- engaging every learner.

As a teacher begins to understand and develop competency in these areas, he or she also
develops a certain level of automaticity, as described in Chapter 1: the ability to act and
react quickly and intentionally to the many unique situations that arise in the classroom
each day. As someone who has most likely been teaching for several years, you have
achieved a level of fluency, or automaticity, that often evades new teachers. It can take a
new teacher years to feel comfortable making the innumerable quick decisions that are
part of each teaching day—not to mention making them in ways that consistently reflect
how the teacher wants to be with children, how the teacher wants them to be with each
other, and how he or she wants the classroom to run.

Your role in getting your student teacher on the path to automaticity is a combination of deepening his or her understanding of the conditions that lead to a caring learning community, showing how those conditions are affected by all kinds of teaching
decisions, and giving your student teacher opportunities to make many, many teaching decisions that he or she can then analyze and talk over with you.

Building Relationships with Students and Families

When a mentoring teacher understands that building caring classroom relationships is the
key to creating a successful learning community, he or she naturally wants the student
teacher to understand the adult's role in seeing that such relationships are developed. But
before a student teacher will be able to influence students' relationships with each other,
his or her first step is to establish his or her own caring relationships with children.

"Perhaps because I got my initial credential in secondary education, I didn't
receive any training in community building. Nobody ever said to me, 'You

need to build relationships with your kids.' They taught me how to teach English. And then when I went into a seventh/eighth grade combination class, I was a disastrous student teacher. I just know that if my cooperating teacher had been aware enough to say, 'Gee, Allison, the real thing here is that you need to build relationships,' it would have made such a difference. Just that—not even the how-to, but just a wake-up—would have helped."
(STUDENT TEACHER)

When Student Teachers Are New in the Role of "Nurturer"

It would seem, on the face of it, that building caring relationships with students should be the *easiest* part of a student teacher's job. After all, most of them choose to go into teaching because they like children and want to help them learn. Because of their youth, however, most student teachers' experience in forming relationships has been with equals, such as friends, or with superiors, such as mentors, teachers, and parents, who take a nurturing stance toward them. Few student teachers have had much experience forming warm, caring relationships in which they themselves are primarily responsible for nurturing the other person. They will often need help understanding this kind of relationship and their role in it. Such relationships are not based on enjoying the other, as in peer friendships, nor on gaining help or nurturance from the other, as in mentoring relationships. Instead, they require that the student teacher be strong enough to sustain the relationship even if a particular child is not enjoyable, that the student teacher take the initiative to build the relationship even if a particular child rejects his or her efforts, and that the student teacher figure out how to meet the child's needs and how to help the child contribute to the relationship. In short, teacher-student relationships require more patience, perspective-taking skills, resilience, and persistence on the part of the adult than most new teachers are accustomed to.

> "I've learned that it really helps to establish a relationship with each kid as much as possible. You can't just show up and teach and not worry about what the students are thinking of you—not if you want them to pay attention to you." (STUDENT TEACHER)

A common "mistake" is for student teachers to try to be friends with children—treating them as equals and trying to please them in every way. Sometimes this results in failing to challenge students to meet increasingly higher standards of learning and behavior. Sometimes the affection a student teacher receives from children leads him or her inadvertently to nurture children's dependence rather than to encourage their independence. And sometimes, in this friendship mode, a student teacher is so hurt by a particular child's rejection that he or she comes to resent and dislike the child—rather than take the responsibility to work through the difficulties and find a way to form a positive relationship despite all.

> "When I was a student teacher I was teaching a middle school combination class, and I was there to make friends. I was going to be as 'hip' as these kids. And I thought I was. Then they locked me out of the classroom when it was time for my takeover and I was devastated. In retrospect, I can see that they were actually treating me like one of their buddies. They lock each other out of the classroom, too. It was a very clear, very difficult lesson—I'm not there just to make friends." (COOPERATING TEACHER)

When Student Teachers' Backgrounds Are Different from Those of the Students

Another challenge in relationship building arises when student teachers are a different social class or race from their students. First, they may find it difficult to break through their own stereotypes, which often leads to misreading the children's signals and eventually to a general breakdown in relationships. They may also feel so unsure of how to relate to students whose backgrounds are different from theirs that certain children intimidate them, making it impossible to act with authority toward them and thus impossible to form nurturing relationships with them. Another response common among student teachers is to try to compensate for the social injustices the world heaps on some children—by demanding less of them. This response shortchanges children of the appropriate challenges that can help them grow, and by definition precludes the development of nurturing relationships with them.

> "I had come from a small school in a real country setting, and it was almost like shell shock to go from such a rural place to an urban setting. Some of the lessons and approaches that worked in the first school were not effective at all. My cooperating teacher would talk to me about different kids and some of their situations—and their lives were very different from what I had been used to. I had to make some changes and I had to build trust with each child." (STUDENT TEACHER)

> "My student teacher had done a huge study the year before on African-American males and their mistreatment in society. And so I think she had a hard time looking at the boys in my classroom without seeing them as subjects from her research. Her goal seemed to be to have relationships with these particular children, but she pursued it to the exclusion of having high

standards for them. She was honestly trying to engage and grow and learn with the kids, but fundamentally she felt that she could not have traditional goal-setting/consequence conversations with the children because they were already 'at risk' for not having had enough nurturance in society. She never gave up that philosophy, even when the class deteriorated into chaos." (COOPERATING TEACHER)

Inherent Challenges in the Nature of Student Teaching

In addition to these common difficulties that student teachers encounter in trying to build caring and nurturing relationships with students, a few others are inherent in the nature of student teaching. For example, the timing of when a student teacher joins your classroom may be an issue.

A student teacher who joins the classroom at the beginning of the year benefits by being included in the community from the start. He or she is automatically a member of the group as it forms and participates in getting-to-know-you activities and norm-setting meetings (or community circles). But if your student teacher is a newcomer later in the year, he or she walks into an existing community and a well-developed web of relationships. The students are likely to feel less safe, less trusting, and less patient with this newcomer than they do with you, and perhaps even a little resentful of letting a student teacher replace you. After all, they know you, they are used to the ways you handle the classroom, and, most importantly, they trust you.

> "When I started student teaching in January, it was really important to me to bond with the children, but the process seemed slow and I wasn't making the connection. My cooperating teacher suggested checking in with individual students with comments like 'How do you think your day is going so far?' and 'What can we do to help you have a good afternoon?' And she suggested using lunch time—I had already been having lunch with the kids—to seek out the four or five children I was having the most trouble with and talk with them about things other than school. Over time I could see the bonds developing. Disruptions were fewer, and one particular child, who used to say boldly, 'I wish Ms. Lowry was teaching, not you!' started asking me for help and would walk by and give me an affectionate, playful tap on the back while I was working with others. She'd walk right by as if she hadn't done it, and I would just smile and acknowledge her. It was a real breakthrough." (STUDENT TEACHER)

TOOL **6** What You Can Do

BUILD RELATIONSHIPS WITH STUDENTS AND FAMILIES

▶ Help the student teacher reveal himself in ongoing ways.

▶ Help the student teacher create opportunities for children to share about themselves.

▶ Help the student teacher convey to students "we're in this together."

▶ Help the student teacher learn to recognize and treat each child as a special person.

▶ Help the student teacher enjoy the children and be himself in whatever ways feel right for him.

▶ Introduce the student teacher to parents and families.

▶ Facilitate the student teacher's communication with parents and families.

ESTABLISH AUTHORITY AND CONTROL OF THE CLASSROOM

▶ Anticipate that the student teacher will have different needs for power assertion than you do.

▶ Think through with the student teacher how she will handle some typical problem situations.

▶ Encourage the student teacher to choose two or three specific techniques and make a conscious effort to use them until they feel comfortable to her.

▶ Help the student teacher think about ways to exercise power that are less damaging than others to the sense of community.

▶ Let the student teacher take over classroom management in "chunks."

▶ Arm the student teacher with teaching strategies that make the task clear, and so eliminate some potential behavior problems.

▶ Help the student teacher feel more comfortable acting with assurance.

▶ Talk about when it is appropriate to listen to students' concerns about a particular decision.

▶ Have the student teacher observe you for control techniques, and then debrief with her.

▶ Be careful not to let the children pit you and the student teacher against each other.

What You Can Do TOOL6

MAKE THE VALUES CLEAR AND CONSISTENT

▶ Help the student teacher be clear about the ethical principles that frame your classroom.

▶ Explain to the student teacher how classroom procedures reflect the importance of fairness, personal responsibility, kindness, and so forth.

▶ Share and post a list of ideas generated by the children for solving common problems.

▶ Suggest that it is sometimes helpful to introduce the discussion of a problem with a personal story.

▶ Encourage the student teacher to have one-on-one problem-solving conversations with students.

▶ Remind the student teacher to assume the best possible motive for misbehavior consistent with the facts.

▶ Help the student teacher find ways to tap children's intrinsic motivation to be good people and to learn.

▶ Have the student teacher observe the classroom and your interactions with children through a values lens, and then debrief with her.

ENGAGE EVERY LEARNER

▶ Describe how you get children motivated and engaged in learning activities.

▶ Describe how you design lessons to keep students motivated and engaged.

▶ Sit down and co-plan lessons with your student teacher.

▶ "Shadow" the student teacher's teaching.

▶ Use your teaching not as a model but as a text.

In relationships with parents and families, a student teacher's role also is inherently challenging. Not only is the student teacher *not you,* but he or she is most likely both younger than students' parents and caregivers and considerably less experienced with children than they. Your student teacher will benefit from your guidance about how best to relate to children's parents and families. Take time to share the ways in which you have developed relationships and positive communication with them, and help your student teacher understand his or her role as a professional authority in the classroom (even though your student teacher may be young and inexperienced).

WHAT YOU CAN DO — BUILDING RELATIONSHIPS WITH STUDENTS AND FAMILIES

Like all teachers, student teachers need to earn children's trust. You can help your student teacher understand and recognize that he or she has the power to close the distance between him- or herself and the students. You can also model the value you place on helping everyone get to know everyone else better. What follows are some strategies for helping your student teacher focus on building nurturing, authoritative relationships.

1 **Help your student teacher reveal him- or herself in ongoing ways.** In addition to participation in initial welcoming and getting-to-know-you activities that you set up, your student teacher may want to try some of these strategies:

- Spend time playing and talking with children at recess and as they arrive in the morning.

"I noticed when I was observing my student teacher that she wasn't really connecting with the children. For example, in the mornings when the kids came in she tended to busy herself with getting her center ready or filing things away. I mean she literally had her back turned away from the kids. And so I began checking in with her and I said, 'You know, I think the kids really want to hear your voice and get to know you. I would also like it if you could just take five minutes to greet them at the door and make sure they're settled in.'" (COOPERATING TEACHER)

BUILDING RELATIONSHIPS WITH STUDENTS AND FAMILIES

- Invite children to have lunch with him or her in small groups.

- Be real. Listen to kids and empathize: "I understand how you could feel that way" or "I felt that way when I was young."

- Share stories about him- or herself with the class.

- Share favorite books with the class.

"I ate lunch with the kids every day. I took turns sitting at different tables and talking with them." (STUDENT TEACHER)

"I shared something personal about myself and my life with the children. They were curious and asked me a lot of questions. It felt natural and important." (STUDENT TEACHER)

2 **Help the student teacher create opportunities for children to share about themselves.** The good news is that most children love to tell adults stories about their lives. If your student teacher is having trouble creating such opportunities, you might suggest that he or she try the following:

- Collect information to help introduce a conversation. For example, greet and talk with children's parents and siblings; get to know children's neighborhoods; learn where children live.

- Ask questions about what's going on in their lives and then take time to hear about soccer games, special trips, new pets, hard times, visiting grandparents, and so forth.

- Ask children to bring in a picture of something or someone they love and have them share it with the class.

WHAT YOU CAN DO   BUILDING RELATIONSHIPS WITH STUDENTS AND FAMILIES

3 **Help the student teacher convey to students "we're in this together."** Your student teacher might do this in the following ways:

- Convey that problems that arise in the classroom are something for everyone to solve together.

- Set an expectation that everyone helps everyone until everyone is finished, especially when hard work needs to be done.

- Point out the ways in which the class has grown or improved over time.

- Start participating right away in community circle time or class meetings.

- Celebrate successes and good times as a class—not as a reward but as an acknowledgment of what has been achieved.

"My student teacher remembered it was our one-month anniversary of her being in the classroom, so she put together a little celebration. The kids were surprised, delighted, and laughed together at the way it sounded as though they had 'married' her!" (COOPERATING TEACHER)

BUILDING RELATIONSHIPS WITH STUDENTS AND FAMILIES | WHAT YOU CAN DO

4 Help the student teacher learn to recognize and treat each child as a special person with unique needs, talents, experiences, and perspectives (it's at the heart of good teaching). If your student teacher could benefit from help in this area, spend some time talking about individual children and their unique needs, challenges, and contributions. You may also want to suggest some of the following ideas:

- Spend time with children individually—over a book, over lunch, over a break between activities—and try to reach every child on some level.

- Ask children to create a whole-class "About Me" book or perhaps a class quilt.

- Invite children to write in their journals what they would like you (the student teacher) to know about them, what they enjoy about class, what they want to change. Collect and read the journals, and write back to students on a regular basis.

"I felt really comfortable building relationships with the kids. I just made a point of connecting with each child. But there was one child I was thinking about at the end of the semester, and I realized on the very last day before the winter break that I had missed him—I had let Eric slip past me. For whatever reason, over the whole semester, he's the one student I just didn't come to know much about. It really caused me to wonder, how did I do that? How did that happen? Because I tried really hard to spend one-on-one time with every student, as much time as I could within the constraints of teaching to the whole class." (STUDENT TEACHER)

"Students really opened up in their journals. They wrote about pressure from their peers and in their communities. They wrote about problems they were having at home and with friends. I really came to know my students through their journals—so much better than any other way. The journals made them real people to me." (STUDENT TEACHER)

"When kids were having trouble lining up, I had them do it over and over until they got it right. They missed a special P.E. event because of the time it took and they were upset about that. So I had them write me letters about how they felt

WHAT YOU CAN DO BUILDING RELATIONSHIPS WITH STUDENTS AND FAMILIES

about the whole situation. I took all of those letters home and wrote back to them. After that experience I decided to recommend that whenever they wanted to write about anything, they could write in their journals to me and I would answer them back. This ended up helping so much. They started writing about lots of things. Some of them wrote requests such as, 'I'm having a hard time concentrating in my seat because the people around me are talking too much.' Later on I also got some positive comments. One child wrote, 'I really like what you are doing. Can you stay longer?'" (STUDENT TEACHER)

- Remember that all children have basic needs for autonomy, belonging, and competence, and that their unacceptable behavior is usually the result of not knowing how to get their needs met. They may believe, for example, that they cannot succeed unless someone else fails, or that their competence must be measured against someone else's incompetence, or that their group membership depends on excluding someone else. In most cases, it is children's lack of understanding and limited repertoire of behaviors and skills that are problematic, not the children themselves.

"I noticed that I began to try to see them [the children] as individuals and as puzzles rather than as obstacles." (STUDENT TEACHER)

"Even when we assume that kids do want to belong to a caring community, there may be other things going on with them—things having nothing to do with your efforts. Student teachers need to be very attuned to this because in our great fervor to create a just and caring community, we have to remember that it takes a lot of work to get there. There will be times when kids will be showing you behaviors that are the complete opposite of what you want—even after you've started laying the groundwork for a caring community. I think student teachers get surprised when their good intentions aren't reflected right back. You can be the kindest, nicest, fairest teacher in the world, but you will have some kids who continually disappoint you because they are reacting, not to you, but to what has happened in their lives up to now,

BUILDING RELATIONSHIPS WITH STUDENTS AND FAMILIES | **WHAT YOU CAN DO**

and what's happening in their lives outside of school at the moment." (COOPERATING TEACHER)

- Try to focus on something likable about each child.

"My student teacher has decided to give out two special thank-yous at the end of each day, and by the end of ten days she will have given one to each student. The children love it and clap for each other. I think the whole class gets her message—'Yes, I know you! I know who you are!'—and they all know that she has something positive to say about each of them." (COOPERATING TEACHER)

- Make notes about every child based on observations and personal interactions (see Tool 3: Information Exchange for more detail).

5 Help the student teacher enjoy the children and be him- or herself in whatever ways feel right. Share examples of how having a sense of humor or being yourself have carried you through.

"After working only in suburban schools, my student teacher chose specifically to work in an urban school. When she got to my classroom, it was different for her, plus my kids were a difficult group to manage and keep focused. To build her confidence, we decided that initially she would just do the start-the-day routines—calendar, weather, and greeting individual children—until she could stop worrying about the procedures and relax enough to be herself, enjoy the kids, and pay attention to what they were saying and doing and needing." (COOPERATING TEACHER)

6   **Introduce the student teacher to parents and families.** Introduce the student teacher to parents and families in person as well as in a letter or class newsletter, and encourage him or her to communicate with parents right from the start.

> "I introduce each of my student teachers to families in our class newsletter, and I encourage the student teachers to make a round of phone calls to parents to establish a relationship. The children know that the student teacher can call parents just as easily as I can—to share news, something positive that has happened, or a problem. And this way, if something happens with a particular child during the takeover, I'm not the one to call."
> (COOPERATING TEACHER)

7   **Facilitate the student teacher's communication with parents and families.** Encourage your student teacher to talk informally with parents or caregivers when they bring their children to school in the morning or pick them up at the end of the day. Include your student teacher in a professional role during back-to-school night, conferences, and other school functions.

> "At parent–teacher conferences I was running late, so my student teacher went out to talk to the parents in the hallway. She asked questions about their children and told parents about the special little things she's noticed or conversations she's had with their children. Months later an unusually demanding parent told me that it had made a big difference to her." (COOPERATING TEACHER)

Establishing Authority and Control of the Classroom

Although children in a caring community are given a lot of responsibility for their own learning and relationships, the teacher plays a critical role in maintaining control. Children need to know that they are safe—that the teacher, as an authority, will not allow bad things to happen in the classroom. The more children feel confident that they won't get hurt and the more they feel safe from teasing, put-downs, and bullying, the more they experience a sense of belonging—and the more they can focus on learning. As an experienced teacher, you understand this dynamic. An important part of your role is to help your student teacher understand it as well and to help him or her learn some of the skills that make it possible.

When Student Teachers Underplay the Need for Control

All teachers struggle to establish the "right" level of control, but for student teachers the struggle is intensified. Their inexperience being the nurturer in relationships often leads them naively to believe that control isn't necessary, to resent children when it *is* necessary, and to believe that requiring certain behaviors of children unduly limits their autonomy. Additionally, they may have a strong aversion to the *idea* of control. For many of us, the connotations of "control" and "authority" are negative. Images of stern, didactic teachers bent on dominating children come to mind. No student teacher would hope to become a "controlling" teacher. Without your help, your student teacher may fail to understand that he or she can be caring *and* strong, flexible *and* consistent, child-centered *and* in control, and that he or she can be fair precisely *because* of being the classroom authority.

Student teachers will be especially sensitive to the necessary tensions of letting children know right from the start that as the classroom leader they are in control, that what they say goes, and that at the same time they are fair and reasonable. Student teachers will also quickly be struck by the inherent tensions between meeting each child's need for autonomy and their own need to exercise reasonable control. They will need to sort out how to maintain a friendly relationship with a child while preventing the child from behaving in disruptive ways and how to foster a student's sense of personal competence while requiring that the child perform better. Student teachers often need help understanding and balancing these tensions.

> "At first I didn't value the idea of having control of the class, because I wanted children to feel that it was their classroom. Now I see that kids really need to know that you're running the show—that as the teacher, I am in control. They may have many real choices in the classroom—

about the direction of their science experiment, or what book they're going to read—but they know that I'm in control in relation to their physical and emotional safety. That control often comes from the ability to very quickly quiet the class down or make them sit in their seats very still and calmly. I used to dismiss that kind of control as military, but now I see that there has to be a high enough level of control that students know you aren't going to let others laugh at them or hurt them." (STUDENT TEACHER)

"Student teachers don't yet have individual connections with students, so they need to connect with the whole group. My student teacher did a lot of unity-building activities. For example, she brought in muffins on the first morning, and she had kids make puzzle pieces about themselves and as a class put the pieces together. But she also mentioned that she is introducing herself to parents over the phone and will call them to share what's going on in the classroom. So she's building relationships all the time, but also letting students know that there's some accountability." (COOPERATING TEACHER)

When Student Teachers Resort to Power Assertion

Despite wanting to avoid blatant power assertion, student teachers often talk about the chaos in their classrooms that prevents them from teaching. When students sense that the student teacher is "less powerful" than the experienced teacher, it creates an opening for unfocused and even outrageous behavior. Thus, student teachers may need to overemphasize their power to compensate for the gap. Those who become stricter—who, in essence, act with more power—seem to experience greater success as student teachers.

"Things were out of control for a while and we were wasting a lot of time. I was getting aggravated and the kids were unhappy. So the way it was going was not really serving anybody. Though it's definitely not my goal or desire to have names on the board, I did it and have no regrets about doing it because it worked much better. And if I were in the same situation again, where I didn't think anything was getting done, I would do it again. But I would continue to strive to do other things so that I wouldn't have to stay at that stage." (STUDENT TEACHER)

ESTABLISHING AUTHORITY AND CONTROL OF THE CLASSROOM   **WHAT YOU CAN DO**

As the cooperating teacher, there are some things you can do for your student teacher to ease him or her into an authoritative role. A bigger challenge is to help your student teacher exercise whatever power he or she needs to keep the classroom running successfully, while also helping your student teacher grow into the kind of teacher who can use less power over time because he or she has a variety of other strategies that provide alternative ways to be in control.

1 **Anticipate that the student teacher will have different needs for power assertion than you do.** Even though you may not use extrinsic control techniques, be prepared that your student teacher may need to. Help your student teacher use them in ways that supplement his or her other efforts to build students' inner commitment to good behavior. If you do use extrinsic control techniques, help your student teacher recognize that these have become just a small part of your approach to classroom management.

2 **Think through with the student teacher how he or she will handle some typical problem situations.** Have your student teacher come up with a list of "what ifs." Offer some of the specific things you do or say, such as dropping rather than raising your voice to get attention, or using physical proximity rather than reprimands to help a student focus. By having anticipated with your help what might happen and what he or she might do—during transitions, at dismissal for lunch, or when a learning activity gets chaotic, for example—the student teacher will be ready with a number of options, not all of them dependent on power assertion.

"For everything I planned, I tried to think it through and say to myself, 'What happens if? What am I going to do?' I'd go through a lot of 'what ifs' and have a couple of different plans in mind. I also created a folder of activity sheets so that if I needed to, at any point I could say, 'Okay, everybody, go to your desks. We're going to switch gears.' It became something they were comfortable with—this image of switching gears and going back to desks—and it allowed me to take a break emotionally if I needed it, or to talk to an individual student." (STUDENT TEACHER)

WHAT YOU CAN DO   ESTABLISHING AUTHORITY AND CONTROL OF THE CLASSROOM

3 **Encourage the student teacher to choose two or three specific techniques and make a conscious effort to use them until they feel comfortable.** Once your student teacher has incorporated those techniques, have him or her choose a few more to work on.

"Sometimes student teachers will panic and their minds will go blank. I try to arm them with a mental list of the language of the classroom that children respond to—things like 'Please make a good choice right now' and 'I don't think anyone can do their best work like this' and 'Let's take a break and put our heads on the desk for a minute.'"
(COOPERATING TEACHER)

4 **Help the student teacher think about ways to exercise power that are less damaging than others to the sense of community.**

"When I was having difficulties with a few students, I decided to pull them out individually to talk to them for five or ten minutes outside the classroom while everybody else inside was working. And I would also pull out other students, kids I wasn't having trouble with, because I didn't want to give the impression that I was taking students out and punishing them. I felt it was a good way of checking in with the kids." (STUDENT TEACHER)

ESTABLISHING AUTHORITY AND CONTROL OF THE CLASSROOM   **WHAT YOU CAN DO**

5 **Let the student teacher take over classroom management in "chunks."**
Have your student teacher work first with easily manageable chunks of students. Also, help him or her break the teaching into chunks and handle one teaching chunk at a time. For example, you might take over the morning attendance and paperwork for a week and let the student teacher concentrate on managing the morning meeting.

> "I gave my student teacher the ESL students as her first small-group project because they were a very engaged group of low readers, whereas the rest of the low group was much tougher. This experience was to enable her to learn to teach and see what struggling readers look like without mixing struggling readers with struggling behavior. And once she got her feet on the ground in terms of the teaching, then I integrated the other kids."
> (COOPERATING TEACHER)

> "We tend to start off slow and then, all of a sudden, the snowball starts rolling downhill. I think it has been important for me as a mentor teacher to control that snowball as much as possible and not hand over too much too fast. This way, my student teacher can get comfortable running the classroom in manageable chunks." (COOPERATING TEACHER)

6 **Arm the student teacher with teaching strategies that make the task clear, and thus eliminate some potential behavior problems.** Suggest some of the following:

- Lead a role-play before an activity to show students exactly what it should look like.

- Have students model an activity before the class undertakes it.

WHAT YOU CAN DO   ESTABLISHING AUTHORITY AND CONTROL OF THE CLASSROOM

- Before an activity, talk over with students what it will mean for them to be responsible (or helpful or kind or respectful) during the activity you are introducing.

7 **Help the student teacher feel more comfortable acting with assurance.**
Impress on your student teacher the need children have for him or her to act decisively. And assure your student teacher that he or she can change a response later, if necessary.

> "Kids depend on you to be sure, even if you're paddling like crazy underneath." (COOPERATING TEACHER)

> "I try to help my student teacher see that the children are not glass. They're resilient. You can act with confidence and make a mistake, and the kids will be okay. They just need to know that there's accountability and that things are fair." (COOPERATING TEACHER)

8 **Talk about when it is appropriate to listen to students' concerns about a particular decision.** Whether a decision was made on the spur of the moment or with great deliberation, students may have concerns. Contrast the student teacher's choice of being open to concerns raised in a responsible way with the recommendation that he or she refuse to be drawn into whining or complaining.

ESTABLISHING AUTHORITY AND CONTROL OF THE CLASSROOM   **WHAT YOU CAN DO**

9 **Have the student teacher observe you for control techniques, and then debrief what you did.** Have the student teacher try to incorporate some of these techniques into his or her own teaching.

> "I hear my student teacher using my words and inflection, especially when she says some of the exact things I say, such as 'Check your bodies' or 'Fix the problem.' The bottom line is that she's inheriting my classroom midway through the year, and although she laughs at how much she sounds like me, it works. I just want to acknowledge—and she knows this—that what she's learning in my room is just one way, not THE way. I always like to remind her that when she has her own classroom she can do some of what I do but also discover her own ways." (COOPERATING TEACHER)

10 **Be careful not to let the children "split the system."** Students can be quite masterful at playing you off against your student teacher. Talk over how you will handle situations in which this is likely to happen. Your collegial relationship as well as your authority could be at stake.

> "One day the student teacher was tutoring children after school and when I walked in, three boys immediately asked, 'Can we have a snack?' The student teacher quickly said no because they had already asked her. She made it clear to them that she was an authority. If she hadn't done that quickly, I would have answered the boys and inadvertently undermined the student teacher's authority." (COOPERATING TEACHER)

Making the Values Clear and Consistent

Children need to experience fairness, respect, helpfulness, responsibility, honesty, and kindness in order to reciprocate such behavior. But they also need guidance in talking about why these core values are important, how they relate to specific behaviors in the classroom, and how these values can be applied broadly in the world.

In addition to formal opportunities to talk with children about values, hundreds of informal opportunities pop up in the classroom each week. Student teachers have much to learn about how these values manifest themselves in the classroom and how to respond when they do (or do not).

Making Sure That Core Values Are Understood and Applied

As a cooperating teacher, you will want to make sure to take the time to explain how you have worked to incorporate values into your classroom. These are not values about which you and your student teacher can afford to disagree. A student teacher may not value neatness or quiet or spontaneity or humor as much or as little as you do—and any problems working out such values will need to be negotiated—but the core *ethical* values that guide your practice are not negotiable, so it is essential that you help your student teacher see their importance.

Another challenge for you is helping the student teacher understand how these core values relate to his or her own behavior. If the student teacher's own actions in the classroom are not congruent with the values he or she emphasizes for students, children will quickly pick up on any inconsistencies. They are especially concerned with whether the student teacher is going to be "fair," and whether he or she can explain why something is fair when it may not be readily apparent to them.

> "What bothers the kids during the student-teacher takeovers is when things aren't fair. They don't like it when one student gets in trouble and one doesn't, and they plead for fairness. We teachers are old hands at managing fairness and being very straight with kids. We tell them, 'This is why I'm letting you do it and not him.' And you can take them through your process. But it comes from years of head banging and finally being clear about it in your own mind." (COOPERATING TEACHER)

While agreeing on core ethical values, you or the student teacher may believe that some aspect of a value needs a stronger focus. For example, one of you might think that upholding the value of fairness requires special attention to issues of gender or a concern for racial equity. One of you might be sensitive to how competition can create inequitable access to the curriculum. It is important for you to be open to the values and insights a student teacher may bring, for the student teacher to be open to your ideas, and for both of you to be able to discuss these issues comfortably.

Predictable Ways in Which Student Teachers Struggle with Values

Student teachers may struggle in several ways trying to apply core values in their practice. First, they may not fully understand or have confidence in their values. For example, they can't waver about whether being responsible is equally important for all students. They can't be discretionary in the kinds of put-downs that get dealt with. They must understand that rationalizing insufficient effort is not a kindness.

A second challenge is to be able to see clearly the many ways that core values apply in daily classroom life and to help students see them as well. Student teachers need to communicate the expectations of the classroom on a daily basis. At the practical level, for example, this might mean reminding students that teasing is absolutely not acceptable in the classroom. On a moral level, it might mean helping students see the short- and long-term effects of teasing on individuals and the community. Developing the antennae that allow student teachers to recognize classroom incidents as opportunities for helping students apply moral concepts is especially challenging when student teachers are just learning how to manage all the other split-second demands of classroom life as well.

> "It's not just the direct teaching you do about values, it's those 'little moments' that come up in the middle of a lesson. And it's the way you respond when a child breaks one of the norms of the classroom."
> (COOPERATING TEACHER)

A third challenge for student teachers is to see the complexity of balancing multiple values. As the cooperating teacher, you may need to guide your student teacher if a particular value is in the way of other values. For example, a student teacher may believe that the value of kindness requires him or her to bend over backward for a poor or disadvantaged child, but fail to see that other children are being harmed by the resulting lack of availability to them and their needs. In other instances, for example, a student teacher may not recognize when honesty should give way to kindness or what to do when respect and honesty appear to be in conflict.

Finally, student teachers will struggle to be consistent in applying core ethical values. To them, this may mean handling similar problems in similar ways. More experienced teachers, however, know that the place for consistency is in the goals of the teacher and the outcomes for students, not in the methods that are applied.

"I see it as being consistently inconsistent at a higher level. It may sound like a contradiction, but I think it's important to find ways to put forth your values and expectations in a manner that is tailored to individual students and their needs. Doing what's 'fair' and 'right' for all children isn't equal necessarily to doing the same thing for all. The reason I send Amanda to the office and the reason I don't send Matthew are the same—but the actions are different." (COOPERATING TEACHER)

WHAT YOU CAN DO   MAKING THE VALUES CLEAR AND CONSISTENT

Beyond helping the student teacher understand the values that operate in your classroom and what that looks like in daily classroom life, you will likely find yourself explaining ways you apply values that may look inconsistent to the student teacher but that are actually consistent with your expectations for all students.

1 **Help the student teacher be clear about the ethical principles that frame your classroom.** Be explicit about the core ethical values that guide your practice. In the beginning of the year, include the student teacher in any class meetings designed to establish classroom norms. Later in the year, include the student teacher in check-in meetings in which students evaluate how well they are keeping to their norms. If students have not brainstormed a list of behaviors that demonstrate the application of these values, make such a list with your student teacher. And encourage your student teacher to find ways to remind students of the behaviors that go along with showing that these values are at work.

2 **Explain to the student teacher how classroom procedures reflect the importance of fairness, personal responsibility, kindness, and so forth.** Some procedures may be classroom routines, such as how class jobs are arrived at. Others involve your approaches to solving classroom problems.

"Fairness is really important in the classroom. I encourage my student teachers to make that clear to the children. For example, one of the ways I do this is when I'm disciplining a child. I often stop and ask the student, 'Am I being unfair?'

MAKING THE VALUES CLEAR AND CONSISTENT

> If he says yes, then I ask more about it, and I know I have to do some thinking. If the student says no, then I know he has to do some thinking."
> (COOPERATING TEACHER)

3 **Share and post a list of ideas generated by the children for solving common problems.** In addition to the class norms students may have generated, you are likely to have had them help identify ways to address typical classroom and playground issues. Encourage the student teacher to turn to this list when problems arise and to revisit with students their problem-solving ideas.

4 **Suggest that it is sometimes helpful to introduce the discussion of a problem with a personal story.** Whether the student teacher is talking about a problem with the whole class or one or two students, help him or her understand how describing a relevant situation from his or her own childhood can defuse students' defensiveness and help them feel comfortable with the problem and with the student teacher.

5 **Encourage the student teacher to have one-on-one problem-solving conversations with students.** Explain the value of taking a student aside or setting up a private meeting to engage the student in solving a problem the student is having or causing. Let the student teacher in on some ways you may open a problem-solving conversation—for example, "How would you like to solve this problem? You're not in trouble, but I need to know that the problem will be solved."

> "I think one of the most powerful moments you can have is when a kid does something crummy and you have a one-on-one talk—not a lecture, but a talk—'What's going on?' 'What happened?' 'You know, I can understand how you might feel. I've felt that way before.'" (COOPERATING TEACHER)

WHAT YOU CAN DO **MAKING THE VALUES CLEAR AND CONSISTENT**

6 **Remind the student teacher to assume the best possible motive for misbehavior, consistent with the facts.** Your student teacher should understand that his or her first duty is to stop any misbehavior (the kind that is harmful), but that his or her second duty is to find out why a student misbehaved. A powerful rule of thumb to share with a student teacher is to assume that a student's misbehavior is a result of the best possible motive consistent with the facts—a misunderstanding, a lack of skill or experience, carelessness—and not to assume and respond to a more negative motive. Student teachers may find this approach a challenge to apply consistently (after all, who doesn't?), but it is a worthy goal in classrooms and in life.

7 **Help the student teacher find ways to tap children's intrinsic motivation to be good people and to learn.** Unless you point it out, your student teacher may not see the importance of intrinsic motivation, let alone how to tap it. Talk about why involving students in norm setting and problem solving helps them see that it is they, not only you, who prefer a just and caring classroom. Also explain to your student teacher how you tap intrinsic motivation in learning activities—the techniques you use both to connect learning to students' previous experience and background knowledge and to help them see the relevance of learning and set a purpose for it. Talk also about your reasons and strategies for avoiding extrinsic motivators such as rewards, prizes, and praise.

8 **Have the student teacher observe the classroom and your interactions with children through a values lens, and then debrief what you did.**

> "My cooperating teacher was a great help in pointing out the moral development side of things—in helping me decide what was right and what wasn't, because I was really struggling."
> (STUDENT TEACHER)

Engaging Every Learner

One of the main reasons you take such care in creating a classroom community is to provide a positive culture so that students can do their best learning. As a cooperating teacher, you will want to help your student teacher see how best to take advantage of the climate for learning that you have established. This is likely to mean helping your student teacher recognize what motivates students to want to learn as well as appreciate what constitutes an effective learning experience.

> "It makes a huge difference what kinds of activities you give kids to do.
> If an activity is interesting, and they feel that there's a reason for them to
> do it, they'll be more likely to do it." (STUDENT TEACHER)

Your student teacher will have received a lot of instruction in his or her teacher preparation program on the topics of curriculum and curriculum planning. In these areas your student teacher may even feel more knowledgeable than an experienced teacher, such as yourself, if you have not taken curriculum-focused university coursework in several years. While you won't want to dampen your student teacher's enthusiasm for introducing curriculum ideas into your classroom, and while you will want to be open to learning about new curriculum ideas your student teacher may offer, you will also want to be sure that your student teacher's plans are in sync with your goals for your students and that his or her ideas about what constitutes engaging curriculum applies to all students, not just the most able or most compliant.

For student teachers, the need for curriculum that engages students is perhaps the aspect of teaching that is easiest for them to understand. It should not take too many minutes into a poorly conceived lesson to realize that the lesson—not the bored or confused or misbehaving students—is the problem.

> "The kids really enjoyed it when I did writer's workshop. And what I
> found out was that when the students were doing things that were really
> interesting to them, then for the most part management was not even an
> issue." (STUDENT TEACHER)

> "For me, classroom management wasn't just being clear about my expectations and demanding it of the children. It was also making sure I felt that
> I had the right to demand their attention, which meant that the activity I
> had for them was worth doing." (STUDENT TEACHER)

WHAT YOU CAN DO   ENGAGING EVERY LEARNER

Beyond explaining what you consider and what you do to engage students, be prepared to offer your own teaching for analysis and to spend the time it takes to co-plan lessons with your student teacher.

1 **Describe how you get children motivated and engaged in learning activities.**
With few exceptions, even well-designed lessons do not automatically communicate why students would want to do them. Help your student teacher understand that there are some things he or she can do to pique students' interest in a lesson or at least convince them of reasons to give a lesson their attention. You may want to suggest any of the following ideas:

- Use introductory activities to help children make personal connections with a topic or story. For example, invite them to describe experiences that are related to the topic or theme that they are about to explore (you also may want to offer stories of your own from time to time).

- Document in a class list students' relevant prior knowledge.

- Introduce any background knowledge that can bridge from what students already know to what they will be learning.

- Have students brainstorm a class list of questions they hope to have answered as a result of the activity or lesson or study.

- Help students brainstorm what might be the purpose of what they are about to learn or its relevance to their future.

ENGAGING EVERY LEARNER

2 **Describe how you design lessons to keep students motivated and engaged.**
For example, offer ideas such as the following:

- Make the activity sufficiently open-ended so that students with a range of abilities can enter and succeed at the activity at their own level and pace.

- Build in ways for students to use many different skills, so that some aspect of the activity feels especially satisfying to every student.

- Include choice points for students at various points in the lesson.

3 **Co-plan lessons with your student teacher.** You may find that these planning times are some of the most enjoyable you spend with your student teacher. Your experience and your student teacher's fresh ideas can be a powerful combination. After a lesson you have planned together, debrief it. For example, brainstorm together how you could have made the lesson more interesting for students. Troubleshoot any parts of the lesson that may have gone wrong. Discuss some options for fixing or avoiding such problems in the future.

WHAT YOU CAN DO   **ENGAGING EVERY LEARNER**

4 **"Shadow" the student teacher's teaching.** Sit beside your student teacher and, for example, as he or she facilitates a discussion and you notice that only a few children are responding, remind the student teacher of some strategies for getting more students involved.

> "Sometimes I would ask my student teacher if it would help if I sat beside him and coached him along. One time during a literature discussion, I sat right next to him and whispered, 'Okay, they've all got their hands up, but don't call on anyone because this is a good time to say, "Turn to the person next to you and share what you are thinking."' I was trying to make my suggestions quietly, but of course the kids could hear me. What surprised me was how much they loved it—hearing why a teacher chooses to do various things. So I made no more bones about it. I told them I would be talking to Mr. Rivera throughout the lesson and they were fine with it." (COOPERATING TEACHER)

5 **Use your teaching not as a model, but as a text.** Be willing to offer your teaching as an ongoing case study. Your willingness to open yourself to analysis and reflection is the most important model you can offer.

The Path to "Automaticity"

Because a student teacher is working on so many new fronts at once, he or she can easily be overwhelmed. At the same time that a student teacher is trying to learn how to design curriculum and engage children in meaningful learning experiences, he or she is also trying to learn how to manage classroom logistics, solve playground problems, and attend to the many different needs of twenty or thirty different children—simultaneously.

The automaticity that good teachers develop over time allows them to handle all these various demands quickly and confidently. Not only have they set up centers before, established a system for the bathroom pass, quieted a room without shouting, and introduced volcanoes, but they are accomplished managers and nurturers, models and leaders.

But for student teachers and beginning teachers, nearly every step of every activity or decision needs to be haltingly thought through. This takes time—often, it takes *too much* time. Either the student teacher rushes and as a result misses a crucial step, or the student teacher takes the time he or she needs but loses the students' interest.

Unfortunately, there are only a few things you can do to help your student teacher develop automaticity. This book is full of suggestions for skills you can demonstrate, or topics you can talk about, or reasoning you can offer—but they alone do not develop automaticity. Automaticity develops with experience. Slowly. Often by taking small steps, one at a time. Besides helping your student teacher take on manageable chunks of responsibility or challenge, the other support you can offer is to share with him or her your own path to automaticity and to assure your student teacher that learning to teach is a developmental process. It takes time and practice to develop both the deep understandings and the split-second responses that are necessary to masterful teaching.

> "You know what the key is—and this really worked for me—the key is not to try to do it all at once, but just to start a few things, or one thing, and just to start slowly to bring an idea into your classroom practice."
> (STUDENT TEACHER)

Appendix

A Reflection Guide
for Teachers

A Reflection Guide for Teachers

AS A TEACHER, HOW DO YOU KNOW THAT YOU ARE BEING THOROUGH AND EFFECTIVE in your efforts to create a classroom that fosters children's ethical, social, and intellectual development? And how do you know that your efforts are having the intended effects on your students? This reflection guide offers a series of ideas about ways that you can promote children's development in your classroom. It is not a checklist. Please focus primarily on the principles at the top of each page and consider the examples as just some of the many ways the principles might be applied. You may have your own ways of realizing these principles, and your students may respond in a variety of ways to your initiatives. Each page includes space for you to note your own ideas and observations.

Ways I can foster children's ethical, social, and intellectual development in the classroom:

1 Foster a sense of community in the classroom and promote personal relationships that are warm and supportive.

2 Include social and ethical learning as an integral part of the classroom program.

3 Use constructivist teaching practices.

4 Use learning activities that are designed to engage students and are open-ended enough for students to find their own level of challenge.

5 Give students fair and equal opportunities to learn.

6 Routinely give students opportunities to exercise their autonomy and responsibility.

7 Foster students' intrinsic motivation, rather than use extrinsic rewards or punishments.

1

Foster a sense of community in the classroom and promote personal relationships that are warm and supportive.

For example, I try to:

■ Project a genuine interest in and liking for all of my students, even those who misbehave or challenge my patience and understanding.

■ Encourage students to discover similarities about themselves and to appreciate and honor differences among themselves.

■ Give students frequent opportunities to plan together and engage in activities that promote classroom unity, spirit, and pride and that positively support their school and local communities.

■ Do things with my students, not to them—for example, solve problems through class discussions, rather than by teacher edict.

■ Avoid distancing myself from my students by, for example, referring to myself in the third person.

■ Share with students meaningful things about my personal life, such as hobbies, interests, and activities.

■ Use inclusive language, such as "our" and "we" when referring to the classroom, materials, and activities.

Other examples:

Indications that my efforts are being successful—for example, students increasingly

■ Appear to be empathic to others and genuinely care about each other.

■ Spontaneously include and invite others into their conversations and activities.

■ Show support for classroom unity and spirit that transcends allegiances to in-groups or cliques.

■ Appear to have a sense of pride in their class and their classroom.

■ Seem to respect me, work with me, and freely come to me to discuss personal concerns.

Other indications:

2

Include social and ethical learning as an integral part of the classroom program.

For example, I try to:

■ Invite students to discuss and explore prosocial values—such as responsibility, helpfulness, and kindness—as an integral part of academic lessons.

■ Encourage students to work collaboratively and help them understand how to treat each other fairly and considerately.

■ Encourage students to discuss, reflect on, and seek help with their social as well as their academic problems.

■ Offer students frequent opportunities to engage in prosocial activities on the classroom, school, and community levels.

■ Offer students frequent opportunities to develop their understanding of and empathy for people of diverse cultures, ages, and backgrounds.

■ Help and encourage students to understand the thoughts, feelings, motives, and perspectives of others.

■ Help students to understand the reasons for rules and procedures.

■ Demonstrate and model by words and deeds my commitment to the principles of kindness, fairness, and responsibility.

Other examples:

Indications that my efforts are being successful—for example, students increasingly

■ Help each other and work with each other in a productive manner.

■ Engage in acts of kindness and include others in activities and conversations.

■ Listen and respond to each other respectfully.

■ Avoid putting each other down or making fun of each other and remind other students not to do so.

Other indications:

3

Use constructivist teaching practices.

For example, I try to:

■ Help students connect new experiences, information, or ideas to their prior knowledge or experience.

■ Focus most instruction on developing students' conceptual understanding.

■ Routinely ask students questions that stimulate their thinking and build their understanding, rather than questions that merely assess their knowledge (for example, that look for the "right" answer).

■ Encourage students to try to solve problems by engaging in trial-and-error explorations based on their own understanding, rather than simply following memorized procedures.

■ Encourage students to ask questions about and explore topics in which they are personally interested.

■ Frequently encourage students to reflect on their own learning.

Other examples:

Indications that my efforts are being successful—for example, students increasingly

■ Demonstrate an interest in and responsibility for their own learning by asking their own questions and suggesting directions for exploration.

■ Spontaneously link ideas to other ideas and to their own knowledge and experience.

■ Appear to accept mistakes as a natural part of the learning process.

Other indications:

4

Use learning activities that are designed to engage students and are open-ended enough for students to find their own level of challenge.

For example, I try to:

- Connect learning activities to a purpose or idea that students can see as meaningful.

- Encourage students to pursue their own interests and explore answers to their own questions.

- Use learning activities that require genuine intellectual effort, yet allow most or all students to find a successful way to complete them.

- Offer students opportunities to approach assignments in ways that allow them to incorporate their own ideas, interests, observations, and experiences into their work.

Other examples:

Indications that my efforts are being successful—for example, students increasingly

- Appear to be intensely focused on their work and express interest and excitement about learning activities.

- Are persistent in their efforts, and are less inclined to become easily discouraged with a task.

- Take the time to complete the assignment to their satisfaction, rather than merely racing to get the job done.

- Appear to take pride in their work.

Other indications:

5

Give students fair and equal opportunities to learn.

For example, I try to:

- Give all students an equal opportunity to contribute to and benefit from class discussions and activities, even though they come to the classroom with different experiences, skills, aptitudes, and customs.

- Give students opportunities to use different skills and talents—for example, analytical, graphic, musical, interpersonal—in completing classroom activities.

- Vary the formats for learning activities—for example, whole-class discussions, small-group discussions, partner chats, and silent reflections—so that students with different learning preferences and skills have opportunities to participate comfortably and with confidence. (For example, some students feel comfortable participating in whole-class discussions, while others don't.)

- Make sure that all students see their home culture, language, and experiences reflected in classroom activities.

- Give all students an equal opportunity to participate in discussions and activities—for example, call on girls as frequently as boys, and never exclude students because of their personality.

Other examples:

Indications that my efforts are being successful—for example, students increasingly

- Seem comfortable contributing to discussions and do not appear to be intimidated by other students, by me, or by the classroom or school environment.

- Seem comfortable sharing ideas and experiences about their own lives and culture.

- Appear to value the skills, talents, and differing perspectives of their classmates.

- Undertake new learning activities and make presentations to the class with confidence.

- Avoid "shutting down" and resisting involvement in class activities.

Other indications:

6

Routinely give students opportunities to exercise their autonomy and responsibility.

For example, I try to:

■ Invite students to participate in setting goals for their learning and in evaluating their progress.

■ Invite students to make suggestions that influence the activities and procedures in the classroom.

■ Invite students to participate in establishing class rules and norms.

■ Give students meaningful tasks to perform in the classroom.

■ Offer students choices with regard to learning activities and how to go about completing them—for example, they can approach assignments in a variety of ways and use different skills.

■ Give students opportunities to practice decision-making skills.

Other examples:

Indications that my efforts are being successful—for example, students increasingly

■ Demonstrate an interest in and responsibility for their own learning.

■ Spontaneously suggest ways to improve their classroom community.

■ Spontaneously take action to support their classroom community—for example, greeting visitors, erasing the board, taking out and replacing materials.

Other indications:

7

Foster students' intrinsic motivation, rather than use extrinsic rewards or punishments.

For example, I try to:

- Help students see the purpose of learning activities and how the activities relate to their own lives.

- Encourage students to work hard for the sake of their own personal growth rather than to get good grades or to do better than others.

- Minimize academic competition among students whenever and wherever possible (for example, never point out the superior performance of one student in an attempt to motivate others; display all students' papers, not just the "superior" ones; and never post or display grades for other students to see).

- Refrain from using stars, stickers, rewards, and other extrinsic motivators to promote academic performance.

- Refrain from giving students points or special privileges for good behavior, or demerits for poor behavior.

Other examples:

Indications that my efforts are being successful—for example, students increasingly

- Seem to be interested in exploring ideas rather than just "pleasing the teacher" or earning credit.

- Express interest and excitement about learning activities.

- Do not seem to be unduly focused on grades or credits.

Other indications:

Teacher Support Materials from Developmental Studies Center

Among Friends: Classrooms Where Caring and Learning Prevail

In classroom vignettes and conversations with teachers, this 210-page book provides concrete ideas for building caring learning communities in elementary school classrooms. With a focus on how the ideas of the research-based Child Development Project (CDP) play out in practice, Australian educator Joan Dalton and CDP Program Director Marilyn Watson take us into classrooms where teachers make explicit how they promote children's intellectual, social, and ethical development. A chapter on theory and research provides a coherent rationale for the approach teachers demonstrate.

The Among Friends Package includes the book, 4 video cassettes visiting 8 classrooms, the Collegial Study Guide, the Teacher Educator Guide, and a packet of 20 teacher reflection guides.

At Home in Our Schools

The 136-page book focuses on schoolwide activities that help educators and parents create caring school communities. It includes ideas about leadership, step-by-step guidelines for 15 activities, and reproducible planning resources and suggestions for teachers. The 12-minute overview video is designed for staff meetings and parent gatherings to create support for a program of whole-school activities. The 48-page study guide structures a series of organizing meetings for teachers, parents, and administrators.

The At Home in Our Schools Package includes the book, the overview video, and the Collegial Study Guide. (Also available separately.)

Blueprints for a Collaborative Classroom

This 192-page "how-to" collection of partner and small-group activities is organized into 25 categories that range from quick partner interviews to complex research projects. Over 250 activity suggestions are included for all elementary grades. In addition, Fly on the Wall vignettes offer insights from real classrooms.

The Blueprints for a Collaborative Classroom Package includes the book, an overview video, 3 video cassettes visiting 6 classrooms, the Collegial Study Guide, the Teacher Educator Guide, and a packet of 20 teacher reflection guides.

Choosing Community: Classroom Strategies for Learning and Caring

In 9 videotaped presentations, author and lecturer Alfie Kohn describes pivotal choices that promote community and avoid coercion and competition in classrooms. A 64-page facilitator's guide for use in staff development accompanies the presentations, which include such topics as "The Case Against Competition," "The Consequences of 'Consequences,'" "The Trouble with Rewards," and "Beyond Praise and Grades." The package also includes Kohn's influential book *Punished by Rewards: The Trouble with Gold Stars, Incentive Plans, A's, Praise and Other Bribes.*

Homeside Activities (K–6)

Seven separate collections of activities by grade level help teachers, parents, and children communicate. Each 128-page collection has an introductory overview, 18 reproducible take-home activities in both English and Spanish, and suggestions for integrating the activities into the classroom. The 12-minute English overview video is for parent gatherings and can be used in staff development (as can a 31-minute version). A separate Spanish overview video is specifically designed for parent meetings. The 48-page study guide structures a series of teacher meetings for collegial study.

The Homeside Activities Package includes 6 books (one each grades K–5), the overview video, the study guide, and a 31-minute video visiting 3 classrooms and parents working at home with their children. (Also available separately, as are the grade 6 book and the Spanish overview tape.)

Number Power (Grades K–6)

Each of nine 192-page teacher resource books offers 3 replacement units (8–12 lessons per unit) that foster students' mathematical and social development. Students collaboratively investigate problems, develop their number sense, enhance their mathematical reasoning and communication skills, and learn to work together effectively. (Grades K, 1, 4, 5, and 6 have one volume each; grades 2 and 3 have two volumes each.)

Reading, Thinking & Caring: Literature-Based Reading (Grades K–3)

A children's literature program to help students love to read, think deeply and critically, and care about how they treat themselves and others. Teaching units are available for over 100 classic, contemporary, and multicultural titles. Each 3- to 10-day unit includes a take-home activity in both English and Spanish to involve parents. Also available are grade-level sets and accompanying trade books.

Reading for Real: Literature-Based Reading (Grades 4–8)

A literature-based program to engage the student's conscience while providing interesting and important reading, writing, speaking, and listening experiences. Teaching units are available for 120 classic, contemporary, and multicultural titles, and each 1- to 3-week unit includes a take-home activity to involve parents. Also available are grade-level sets and accompanying trade books.

Reading for Real Collegial Study

Videotaped classroom vignettes illustrate key concepts and common stumbling blocks in facilitating literature-based classroom discussion. A 64-page study guide structures collegial study meetings about "Reflecting and Setting Goals," "Responding to Students," "Handling Offensive Comments and Sensitive Topics," "Guiding Students' Partner Discussions," and "Assessing Student Progress."

That's My Buddy! Friendship and Learning across the Grades

The 140-page book is a practical guide for two buddy teachers or a whole staff. It draws on the experiences of teachers from DSC's Child Development Project schools across the country. The 12-minute overview video is designed for use at staff meetings to build interest in a schoolwide buddies program. The 48-page study guide structures a series of teacher meetings for collegial study and support once a buddies program is launched.

The Collegial Study Package includes the book, the overview video, and the study guide. (Also available separately.)

Ways We Want Our Class to Be: Class Meetings That Build Commitment to Kindness and Learning

The 116-page book describes how to use class meetings to build a caring classroom community and address the academic and social issues that arise in the daily life of the elementary school classroom. In addition to tips on getting started, ground rules, and facilitating the meetings, 14 guidelines for specific class meetings are included. The 20-minute overview video introduces 3 kinds of class meetings. The 48-page study guide helps structure a series of teacher meetings for collegial study. In-depth video documentation shows 7 classrooms where students are involved in planning and decision making, checking in on learning and behavior, and problem solving.

The Collegial Study Package includes the book, the overview video, the study guide, and 99 minutes of video documenting 7 classrooms. (Also available separately.)